LOST CAS
OF ESSEX

David Neville

IAN HENRY PUBLICATIONS

ISBN 0 86025 520 4

Dedicated to
Henry George Neville

Published by
Ian Henry Publications, Ltd.
20 Park Drive, Romford, Essex RM1 4LH
and printed by
Gomer Press, Llandysul, Ceredigion SA44 4QL

INTRODUCTION

The title *Lost Castles* does not mean that they cannot be found. At least four of the castles in Essex are tourist attractions, but most are vestiges of their former glory. Colchester is half its original size, Hadleigh is a shell, Hedingham has lost two towers and forebuilding, Mountfitchet is reconstructed and so on. The castles we visit are not fulfilling the purpose for which they were built, *i.e.* to threaten the populace, to be a jail, to house a great lord or to defend a town. It is the history inside the stones that is lost, the stories of the men and women who, over the years lived and died inside these buildings. Hopefully, this book may help to give some answers to what happened so many years ago.

MOTTE and BAILEY
CIRCA 1066

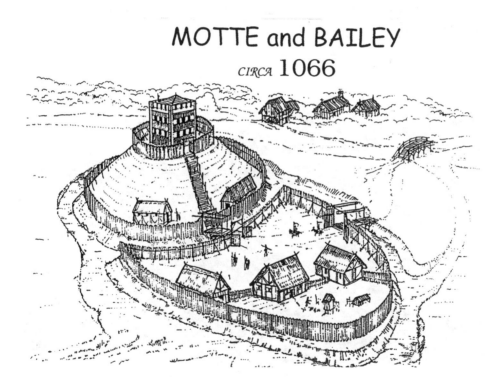

ACKNOWLEDGEMENTS

The following people have been a great help to me with the preparation of this book particularly Mrs Maureen Evens from the Saffron Walden Museum who spent time on the manuscript and gave me much good advice. Also to Stuart Wanfor, work colleague, friend and computer wizard, who helped me find my way around a keyboard and got me out of trouble when things went wrong, which was quite frequently.

To my wife Elizabeth, who put up with books all over the floor for several years, checked dates and spelling, gave me encouragement to continue when difficulties arose and accompanied me when we made frequent trips into muddy fields to see Motte and Bailey castles in all weathers while I rushed around taking photographs.

Also to Guy Petheram and Elizabeth for their help and patience with the final proof readings.

Great Canfield

PREFACE

On 14th October 1066 a catastrophic event took place near the site of the Hoare Apple Tree six miles from Hastings, where Battle Abbey now stands. The shock waves from that day would ripple through England with disastrous consequences. A battle had taken place between the Norman and Saxon armies because William of Normandy challenged King Harold's claim to the throne of England.

The legacies of that day can still be seen around our towns and villages today. England became an occupied country with loss of liberties and rights that the Saxons would never see again. William, later known as 'The Conqueror', systematically set about the complete submission of the populace. He knew that to be accepted as King would be a difficult task; his Norman and French followers, the Knights and Barons who fought at Hastings wanted their reward for victory and the great estates and lands of the Saxon nobility were divided up and given to Normans; this brought home to the population what had happened to their country.

Castles of earth, wood and stone were erected with great haste by the Normans to establish a base from which to govern their newly acquired lands and Essex was no exception. The great names from the 1066 story, Count Eustace of Boulogne, Geoffrey de Mandeville, Aubrey de Vere and many others then were given large estates in the county, and became the principal players in the drama of Norman Essex.

The Normans, using the local Saxons as their workforce, supervised the building of mounds, where possible using existing earthworks or small hills as a base, ideally near streams, or a natural spring for a water supply.

The motte was constructed using earth and shingle in layers with ditches and banks surrounding it. The ditches were usually dry, but some were filled with water to form a moat. On the Bayeux Tapestry, one panel depicts a mound under construction at Hastings; men are seen digging with shovels; the mound shows the layers of earth and shingle and on top is a wooden tower or 'keep' with the word *ceastra* (castle) written. This was the a beginning of castle building in England.

The castles were built about 15 miles apart, a day's patrol for a Norman knight on horseback, this was all part of the plan to subdue the populace and take possession of the land. The Motte supported a timber tower, used as a lookout platform, and, if large enough, the nobleman could live there, away from the noise and smells of the Bailey. The tower, surrounded with a timber palisade, (a fence made of wooden stakes) with a door into the tower itself , was accessed by a wooden staircase on the outside of the earth mound.

The Bailey was at the foot of the Motte, a large area, round or oval in shape, surrounded by a deep ditch and huge palisade. The entrance to the Bailey

3

would be over a drawbridge that spanned the outer ditch and could be pulled up at night for extra security.

In the Bailey were buildings of wood and thatch, where the Norman soldiers lived, alongside their animals and support workforce, men to work in the kitchens, the smithy, and armoury. There were storeage huts for bedding and food, and stables.

The life of this type of castle was short lived because it was vulnerable to attack and especially fire, due to the all-wood construction. Later, strong stonebuilt castles developed. The walls increased in height, and it was easier to defend if attacked or put under siege.

With this increased size the stone castle could accommodate a bigger garrison and living conditions became more comfortable. The motte and baileys were gradually abandoned and the wooden constructions rotted away, leaving the mounds we see today. We know of at least five large motte and bailey type castles from the Norman period in Essex at Ongar, Pleshey, Stansted, Great Canfield and Rayleigh. There are also five other mounds of uncertain date at Stebbing, Great Easton, Mount Bures, Rickling and Elmdon. There were probably others, but over the years erosion and man's development of the land have destroyed their traces. There are earthworks from an important castle at Clavering marked as *site of castle* on the map, and three substantial stone built castles from Norman times at Colchester, Hedingham, Hadleigh, and some small remains at Saffron Walden. We see them today as peaceful places, but they were places of fear for the Saxon and his family.

Four of the motte and bailey castles; Stebbing, Great Easton, Clavering and Mount Bures must be seen from public footpaths as they are on private land; Rickling and Elmdon are not accessible to the public as they are also on private land and unable to be seen from public footpaths.

The exception is Stansted Mountfitchet where you can see a motte and bailey castle reconstructed as is was in Norman times. It is open to the public and a visit is recommended. Pleshey castle can be visited by pre-booking by telephone. The number can be found on a notice board by the castle and you collect the key from a local farm house on the day of your visit. There is a small fee to pay and you get a free leaflet guide. Rayleigh Castle is in the care of the National Trust, you can visit the site at any reasonable time and it is free. The stone castles have regular opening hours, and guide books are available to help you understand the layout and history.

THE HISTORICAL BACKGROUND

It would be helpful at this stage to explain the events pre-Conquest that led to the Normans having an interest in England, the personalities involved, how, and why the castles we see around Britain were built.

In 1042 Edward, the son of Queen Emma and King Æthelred 'the Unready' was summoned to England to be crowned king. The choice of Edward for king needs a brief explanation as he had lived for many years in Normandy, packed off when he was a boy with his brother Ælfred by his mother after her marriage to King Canute in 1017. Emma was the daughter of Richard 'The Fearless', Duke of Normandy, and the sister of Richard II 'The Good', whose second son, Robert was the father of William, later called 'The Conqueror'. Emma was therefore William's great-aunt - the implications of which will become clearer later in the story.

Emma married Æthelred in 1002 when she was very young. Æthelred had been married before, to a lady named Ælgiva, and had a large family of 10 children: six sons and four daughters, but most died in infancy.

When Ælgiva died, Æthelred married Emma in the hope that his new father-in-law would be an ally against the troublesome Danes who, led by Swegn 'Forkbeard', were constantly arriving in England and harassing the people, stealing and looting their goods and cattle, attacking and killing the menfolk. King Æthelred had tried to buy the Danes off with gold to stop the raids: they took the money but always returned even stronger. Then in 1013, England was conquered by Swegn and his son Canute, who drove King Æthelred, his Queen Emma and their children, Edward and Alfred, into exile in Normandy. Swegn was accepted as king, but his reign lasted less than a year, when he suddenly died, causing chaos in the country. Canute left England and returned to Denmark to see his brother.

With Canute out of the country, Æthelred and his Queen returned to England to take back the Crown, with a promise that he would govern the country more competently than before. Canute meanwhile was planning to return and rule England himself. He assembled a great fleet of ships, filled them with fighting men from his native Denmark, and landed in Kent ready to fight for the kingdom that his father had ruled.

To win England was no easy task, as resistance to Canute was to come from the men loyal to King Æthelred. But it was all too much for the King who, with the prospect of more Danish raids, more demands for gold, and fighting to keep his throne, promptly died, probably of exhaustion, in the year 1016. Æthelred's eldest son, from his first wife Ælgiva, Edmund 'Ironside', was however determined to stop the Danish invasion.

He raised an army and bloody conflict ensued for many months. It ended at the battle of Ashingdon in Essex in October 1016, when Canute and Edmund met on the flat land between the river Crouch and the river Roach. The battle raged for many hours until treachery on Edmund's side turned it to Canute's favour. Though many lives were lost that day on both sides, Edmund was able to escape the battlefield and flee to safety.

After the battle Canute and Edmund met to talk peace. An agreement was reached for power sharing by dividing the country with Canute to rule Mercia and Edmund to rule Wessex. This union did not last because Edmund suddenly died, only weeks after the agreement, which was very convenient for Canute as he now became the sole ruler of all England. A strange event now occurred that would have repercussions for the future of England. Emma, the Queen of the late King Ælthelred, suddenly married Canute and became his Queen, despite the age difference Emma being at least 15 years his senior, and the likelihood that Canute was responsible for the early death of her husband. Canute had been married before to Ælfgifu, a lady from Northampton, who had given him two sons, Sweyn and Harold, known as 'Harefoot'. Ælfgifu was sent to govern Norway with her son Sweyn, while Harold remained in England.

Emma's sons, Edward and Alfred, were still living in Normandy with Duke Richard II, so Emma was free to concentrate her time and energy on her new love, Canute. She later had a son, Harthacanute, and a daughter, Gunhild, by Canute, who a great leader and king, uniting for the first time three kingdoms of England, Denmark and Norway. His fear was that when he died his sons would not be able to rule well and hold the kingdoms together; unfortunately he was proved right.

King Canute ruled England for 20 years, building the nation into a strong and independent country. His first act was to create four great earldoms in England - East Anglia, Mercia, Wessex and Northumbria. He then appointed men he could trust to administer these areas. One man, the Saxon Earl Godwin, was given the area of Wessex and later was to become the most powerful man in the country after the King, and whose son, Harold, would become king of the English and be associated with the most famous date in English history, 1066.

Canute died in 1035, leaving a country at peace and well ordered. He had become a Christian and had built many churches. He was respected and feared by the great English and Danish Earls that he had appointed to govern the newly created kingdom. He introduced many sound laws and the country had benefited from them. His death was to cause division in the country for his successor.

His son Harthacanute was in Denmark when his father died. Earl Godwin and Emma were keen to have Harthacanute recalled to England and crowned king, while others favoured Harold 'Harefoot'.

Other candidates were Edward and Ælfred, the sons of Emma and Æthelred, who had travelled from Normandy to visit England. The younger son, Ælfred, was waylaid on his journey at Guildford, and his retainers murdered. Ælfred was taken to Ely and in an act of brutality was blinded, later dying of his injuries. This act was probably carried out on the instructions of Earl Godwin, who did not want any opposition to his own candidate for king. It is not known if Emma, was party to this act Edward returned to Normandy grieving the loss of his brother. The Witan (wise council) meanwhile sent for Harthacanute, who was in Denmark, to offer him the crown, but he failed to respond to their request to return to England, due to problems on the borders of Norway. Meanwhile Harold 'Harefoot', Harthacanute's half-brother, had gained a following and pressed forward his claim for the throne, now supported by the Earl Godwin. He was crowned king in 1035 and was known as King Harold I (not to be confused with Harold II and the battle of Hastings). His first act as king was to banish Emma, as he did not trust her because she had campaigned with Godwin for Harthacanute, and may have been part of the conspiracy in the murder of her own son, Ælfred. Emma went to Bruges, where she lived with Count Baldwin for several years until she was joined by Harthacanute. It is interesting to note that Emma did not go to stay with her brother Robert in Normandy, where her son Edward was staying. There was probably no love lost between mother and son at this time. It must have been many years since they had met.

Edward had lost his brother under tragic circumstances in England, and his mother Emma was under suspicion for his death. The reign of Harold I 'Harefoot' (1017-40) was short lived and unremarkable, he died aged 24 having been on the throne for just five years.

After Harold's death, Emma and Harthacanute arrived on the shores of Kent in a grand show of strength with a fleet of 62 warships.. They were met by Earl Godwin and soon after the country accepted Harthacanute as king.

It is always a problem when great men and leaders like Canute have sons who are expected to have the same qualities of leadership as their father. Sadly this was not the case with Harold I or Harthacanute, who were both weak, vain and cruel men. Harthacanute now accused his ally Godwin of murdering his half-brother, Ælfred, but Godwin denied the charge, in turn accusing Harthacanute's brother - Harold of the crime, and giving the king a gift of a ship and gold. This saved Godwin who continued to serve the king, acting as his representative and supporting the tax collectors, who went into the shires collecting money for the ships the king had acquired from Flanders. This proved very unpopular with the people, who resisted paying the tax. Godwin was forced to use a heavy hand to obtain the funds, and attacked and burnt the city of Worcester when some tax collectors were killed. Harthacanute, in an act of vindictiveness against his dead brother, Harold, had his body dug up and thrown into a river. It was found by local fishermen who reburied the body in secret.

Harthacanute's reign was short lived; drinking at a friend's wedding he went into a convulsive state, falling to the floor shaking violently before he died. He was 24 years of age, and had been king for just two years (1040-42).

Edward, the last of Queen Emma's male children from Ælthelred, was called by the people. His brother Ælfred was dead, as were his half-brothers, and this had left the way clear for Edward. With the backing of Earl Godwin and the English Witan, he was asked to be king, with the hope that the old Saxon line of Wessex would bring stability to the much troubled nation after the turbulent reign of the Danish kings.

Edward was crowned in 1042. He was 40 years old and had lived most of his life in Normandy. He spoke very little English and brought many Norman friends to England with him, including Robert Fitz-Wymarc and Robert, the Abbot of Jumièges: Abbot Robert was to cause problems between Edward and the Godwins later in his reign. King Edward cast a shrewd eye over his new kingdom and consulted with his English earls, mostly members of the Godwin family, who between them were to rule all England in the king's name: Harold of Wessex, Leofric of Mercia, Siward of Northumbria and Gyrth of East Anglia.

The head of the family, Earl Godwin, was most powerful and closest to the king, acting as his advisor in matters of state. Edward's character and upbringing favoured the monastic life of daily prayer. Interested in church matters and piety, he also preferred his Norman friends to Englishmen at court. This was to lead to differences of opinion between Edward and Godwin over policy and promotions. Soon Normans were advising the king and were becoming ministers, much to the disapproval of Godwin and the other English earls. Edward made some ecclesiastical appointments that caused alarm amongst the English hierarchy. His friend, Robert of Jumièges, was made Archbishop of Canterbury over Godwin's choice for the same office, thus weakening Godwin's hold over the king and promoting distrust between Norman and English at court. But Godwin, not a man to be trifled with, had plans of his own. He introduced the king to his daughter Edith, or Eadgyth, whom the king married in the year 1045.

Archbishop Robert used every opportunity to discredit Godwin with the king, and Edward was eager to listen. Things came to a head when Godwin and Count Eustace of Boulogne, a Norman friend of the king, quarrelled over an incident at Dover in 1054 when Count Eustace and his entourage were involved in a brawl with the locals over lodgings for the night. In the fracas several citizens and soldiers were killed. Eustace fled back to London, complained to the King and demanded punishment for the people of Dover, as he was indignant about his treatment there.

Dover was part of the Godwin family lands, so King Edward ordered Earl Godwin to arrest and punish those involved in the skirmish with Count Eustace and his men. Earl Godwin accused Eustace of starting the trouble and refused to chastise his fellow Saxons at Dover. The King was furious with Godwin for disobeying him and summoned him to appear at court to answer charges of disobedience to a King's order. Godwin refused once again to obey the king and called up his men to protect him from arrest by the king's soldiers. Civil war was imminent, Godwin's men at arms against the King's men. After much talking and threats against each other the situation calmed down. The King, who had taken Count Eustace's side over the Dover incident, then banished the Godwin family and confiscated their lands, much to the delight of the king's Norman friends. Harold went to Ireland, and other members of the family went to the continent. In their absence the Normans increased their power at court, which proved unpopular with the people.

Edith, the King's wife, was sent to a nunnery. It was rumoured that the king treated her more like a sister than a wife as he preferred the chaste and holy life to normal married life. There were no children from the marriage, and this raised the question of the succession. With Godwin in exile, Edward's cousin William, the Duke of Normandy, arrived in England to visit the king.

While William was at court the succession was discussed, and Edward may have promised the throne of England to William. This he had no right to do, as the Witan would have to approve any claimants and elections held, but William had in his mind the promise of kingship and the throne of England. When he returned to Normandy this was to be the seed that grew into an obsession that later changed the face of English history forever. Godwin's exile lasted a year. He repeatedly asked Edward to talk about his return to court, but Edward's ear was filled with venom from Archbishop Robert, who hated Earl Godwin and constantly reminded Edward that Godwin was responsible for his brother's death.

Godwin's patience gave way to anger; he gathered men and ships and set sail for England to force Edward to talk terms for his return. He sailed up the Thames gathering support from the people as he went, landing at Southwark to the cheers of the men of London. King Edward hurried to meet Godwin with an army and arranged himself on the north side of the river Thames. The Bishop of Winchester acted as a mediator between the two parties, and a meeting was arranged so that Godwin could state his case and reconcile himself, and his family with King Edward. A large assembly gathered to hear Godwin pledge his loyalty to the king, that was accepted by Edward who restored to Godwin his titles and lands, much to the delight of the Englishmen present at the meeting.

The Frenchmen at the court were not so enthusiastic to see the return of Godwin and made preparations to leave England. Robert of Jumièges, Archbishop of Canterbury, who was disliked by most Englishmen, fled London, going to Clavering Castle, the home of fellow Norman, Robert Fitz-Wymarc (otherwise known as Robert the Staller), and then back to Normandy. Fitz-Wymarc was one of the few Normans that Godwin trusted and he allowed him to stay at court as the king's steward and Master of Horse – the other Normans soon deserted Edward's court.

King Edward the Confessor as depicted in the Bayeux Tapestry

This left the King contemplating his future with Godwin who was by now the most powerful man in England. Edith, Edward's wife, was brought back from the nunnery to rejoin her husband and her father (Earl Godwin) at court. Edward was now under the influence of Godwin who soon promoted Stigand as Archbishop of Canterbury and others he could trust to posts that were once held by Edward's French friends, who were now declared outlaws by Godwin and banned from returning to England. Godwin's sons were given posts of high office and he was hoping that his daughter and Edward might produce a son so that his descendent would some day become king of England.

In 1053 Godwin was feasting with the king, when he suddenly fell to the floor, choking and gasping for breath and died shortly afterwards. Harold, the second son, inherited his father's Earldom, and took over the duties at court. Edward was only too willing to have an able administrator running the country while he concentrated on building his new church on Thorney Island, now known as Westminster Abbey. Harold was an able man, a soldier, diplomat and man of justice, who ruled almost as king while the ageing Edward spent most of his day in prayer and contemplation.

Harold arriving in Normandy

In 1064 Harold and William, Duke of Normandy, met, probably for the first time. Harold was sailing in the Channel, when a storm arose, the tempest driving the ship on to the Norman coast, where Harold and his crew were shipwrecked. They got to the safety of dry land, but were arrested and held in prison by the local Count, Guy of Ponthieu, until Duke William of Normandy was informed of Harold's capture.

Duke William at Beaurain

William arrived to receive Harold, and they rode together to William's castle at Rouen. The two men became friends, Harold even going with William on a campaign to quell a rebellious Norman Count. Harold was unable to leave Normandy and return to England until he agreed to support William's claim to the English throne when Edward died. He was made to swear an oath before he was allowed to return home, but was tricked into swearing on Holy Relics, thus condemning Harold to damnation in the eyes of God if he broke his promise to William. Harold and his retinue were then released to sail back to England. This series of events is depicted on the Bayeux Tapestry, telling the story of William and Harold and the eventual conquest of England.

William and Harold in conference

The year is 1066, the month is January, and the weather is cold, King Edward is wrapped up in bed surrounded by the four people closest to him; he is dying. His wife wraps his feet in her shawl to keep them warm. His head is propped up on the pillow by his friend Robert Fitz-Wymarc. Around the bed stand Harold and Archbishop Stigand. Edward is 64 years old and has reigned for 24 years. Edward then charges Harold to look after his wife Edith and also to look after the nation as king when he is dead, but warns of grave times ahead for Harold and England. As Edward grew weaker his voice became softer, but all those present heard the King clearly state that Harold was to succeed him as sovereign, probably forgetting the promise he made to his cousin William, Duke of Normandy.

King Edward died on 8th January 1066 and was laid to rest the next day in a specially built tomb in his recently consecrated church of St Peter's, Westminster. The Witan then acted on the old king's wish and offered the crown to Harold, who accepted. He was crowned the next day in Westminster Abbey, the first coronation there of a line of Kings and Queens up to the present day. After the coronation Edith retired to Winchester, while Archbishop Stigand and King Harold II stayed in London.

Edward's funeral at St Peter's

Meanwhile across the English Channel in Normandy William was told of Harold's coronation. He became wild with fury as he was expecting to succeed his cousin Edward and be king himself. Harold had promised on holy relics to support his claim with the Witan. Envoys were sent to England on William's behalf to remind Harold of his promise, but Harold replied that he had been chosen by the people and elected by the Witan, as the lawful King of England.

The coronation of Harold II by Stigand

William prepared to take England by force, depose Harold and make himself king. Harold's reign was dogged by problems; a flaming star *(known later as Haley's comet)* had appeared in the sky causing alarm among the people, some claiming it was a bad omen. William's threat of invasion was imminent.

Harold's own brother Tostig had been raiding the south coast after a rebellion in the north, caused by his removal from the post of Earl of Northumbria. He was replaced by Earl Morcar, who had asked Harold to support this move as Tostig was very unpopular in the Northern counties.

In top border of the Tapestry is Haley's Comet

This was approved by Harold, and Tostig was enraged that his brother would not support him and sought help from abroad to reinstate him in his earldom. Harold's troubled reign climaxed in September 1066 when Tostig joined forces with the Norwegian king, Harold Hardrada, who had a vague claim on the throne of England through the old Viking line of King Canute. They sailed up the River Humber and engaged in battle at Fulford with Earls Edwin and Morcar, who were unable to defeat the Viking raiders. Suffering heavy losses they retreated to the city of York, sending messengers to London appealing for help from King Harold. On receiving the news he assembled his army and marched northwards.

Harold Hardrada, Tostig and the Viking army moved towards the village of Stamford Bridge. On 25th September a great battle took place, when King Harold arrived after a forced march and fell unexpectedly on the enemy. Hardrada was killed along with Tostig and most of the Viking force. Harold won a great victory but lost many brave fighting men.

Norman knights and Saxon foot-soldiers

After the battle King Harold and his depleted army went to York with Edwin and Morcar to rest. While this was happening in the north, William, Duke of Normandy, had landed at Pevensey in the south of England. Many ships loaded with men and horses had set sail from Normandy to arrive unopposed on the English shore. Harold received the news of William's landing from a messenger, who arrived in York after riding flat out to reach the king with the bad news. Harold then had to reorganize his army to return to the south and confront William. After a forced march to London, collecting men on the way to bolster his army, and after a brief stay it was onwards towards Hastings where William was camped with his troops.

The famous battle took place and King Harold II lost his life and his kingdom on the slopes of Senlac Hill on 14th October 1066. William, Duke of Normandy, was crowned King of England on Christmas Day of that same year.

The death of Harold

The Normans now ruled; new laws were introduced, castles were built and suppression of the population was implemented. This was a new way of life for the English people, the country was now occupied by a foreign power, their lands taken and given to the new King's allies, large estates were divided up and called manors. Most of the major changes were to affect the upper classes in society and the rich merchants in the towns; to the villager who worked the land the changes came more slowly. There was some resistance to the new rulers, but this was soon dealt with. William would not tolerate any rebellion, and the North of England would suffer the price of defiance. William laid waste to whole areas of land – every village, its animals, crops and ploughs were destroyed, the people killed or moved on. Many people died of starvation or cold with the land unworkable, it took many years to recover.

In 1086 a great survey of the land was carried out as the king wanted to know what was in this land he had conquered. Each village was to submit to the king's commissioners details of each man's wealth, and tax assessment, how many ploughs there were in the village, how many pigs, watermills, woodland, how many skilled men and how many families. The survey was very detailed.

The King's recorders were thorough as they travelled in teams about the countryside, making note of a complete way of life, even who owned the land before Normans came. Over 13,000 villages and towns from all over England were listed in Latin text. Once all the information was collected it was processed and made into several great books, later known as the Domesday Book. These were presented at Salisbury to King William, who acknowledged their contents, and sent them to Winchester for safe keeping. The books were consulted when there were disputes about land and were used by officials in court cases.

William ruled England harshly for 21 years until his death in 1087, and over the years, the people saw many changes, new laws, reforms in the church, and the building of great cathedrals and castles; it became a Anglo-Norman society. The population in England in 1086 was about 2 million, most living in rural areas in small villages or hamlets. Towns like London, Bristol, York and Lincoln were growing fast with the skilled workers in residence and trading and commerce facilities.

This was the last time foreign invaders conquered Britain. The Romans, Angles, Saxons and Jutes, then the Vikings, had all preceded them, but the Normans were the last invaders to settle these shores.

Others in later times threatened to come and preparations were made to meet them. The remains around the coastline of Essex and other areas can be seen today. This book is not about castle architecture; it will only tell you where to find Norman Castles and Motte and Bailey fortifications in Essex, what to see when you get there, and some stories about the interesting characters who lived in those troubled times.

The fortifications at Mountfitchet Motte and Bailey

ONGAR CASTLE
Ordnance Survey Landranger 167   TL 5503

On a wet October day in 1066 the men of Ongar met in the house of Ailid, a freeman and leader of the village. News had reached them telling of the death of King Harold and the great slaughter of their countrymen on Senlac Hill. This disaster must have been the terrible event predicted by the fiery star seen in the sky just after Easter, that had sent them running in fear to the priest at their tiny wooden church in Greensted. The villagers wondered how this bloody defeat by William of Normandy would affect their lives - they were soon to find out.

Walk up Castle Street in Chipping Ongar and you will come to a large artificial earth mound, 50 feet high and 230 feet in diameter, surrounded by water. This is all that is left of the motte and bailey style castle that was a symbol of the military strength of the Norman army, and was used to subdue the Saxons and put fear into the community.

Ongar motte and bailey was built by Eustace of Boulogne, probably over ancient earthworks. He was a powerful Norman baron and had been the brother-in-law to Edward the Confessor, King of England. Count Eustace's first marriage had been to the King's sister Godgifu. Eustace was a frequent visitor to King Edward's court and was responsible for the expulsion and exile of the powerful Saxon family, the Godwins.

Count Eustace of Boulogne was a powerful ally of William, Duke of Normandy, and played an important rôle in the invasion of England with William. Eustace is depicted on the Bayeux Tapestry on horseback, pointing to William as his panic stricken troops started to flee the battlefield when the cry went up that William had been killed.

Eustace and William galloped around to rally the young knights, William with his helmet pushed back to show his face to his troops, and Eustace carrying a Papal banner which had been given to William by Pope Alexander II. The battle raged on throughout the day until the mounted knights broke through the Saxon shield wall, and a combined effort by William's archers and infantry over-whelmed the Saxons protecting Harold, fighting under the Royal standard.

Count Eustace was one of four knights who killed King Harold who was fighting with a battle axe, striking him with their swords until he was dead. As evening fell towards the end of the Battle of Hastings, and while pursuing fleeing Saxons, Eustace was struck in the back by a weapon and was carried wounded from the battlefield. After the battle William and his troops rested at Hastings before moving on to Canterbury, then London.

By the mid-12th century ownership of the castle had passed from Eustace's heirs to Richard de Lucy, a Norman baron. Richard was a supporter of King Stephen (1135-54) then of Henry II (1154-89) and fought for Henry at

Valais in France. He was sheriff of Essex and rose to the rank of Lord Justice of England in 1153. He was also the king's representative when Henry II was in France. Richard was excommunicated by Thomas à Becket for his part in drawing up the Clarendon Constitutions in 1164. This was a document drawn up for King Henry about the relationships between state and church. The clause that Thomas objected to was that stating that if a priest was convicted of a crime by the church court, he should be available for punishment by the state court. The conflict between Henry and Thomas continued until Thomas was murdered at Canterbury in 1170. Henry visited Ongar in 1164 as the guest of Richard de Lucy, who strengthened and enlarged Ongar Castle, also the outer bailey and town enclosure. He also introduced a market or *cheaping* for the community. The town now bears the name Chipping Ongar, the name Ongar is derived from *aungre* the Saxon word for place, so the name means the place of the market. Later Richard resigned all his offices and retreated to a monastery in Kent where he died in 1179. Various owners came and went and the castle was a ruin by the Elizabethan period.

In 1579 William Morice, the then owner, erected a brick house three storeys high on the motte. In time this too fell into decay and was left a ruin. In 1744 Edward Alexander pulled down the ruins of the old house and built a large summer house reached by a winding walk around the motte. This building has also gone, and all we see today is a tree-covered mound surrounded by a water-filled moat. The motte is on private land, but can be seen from the Essex Way footpath, which runs round the edge of the outer bailey to a car park. There is an information board with a diagram of what the castle may have looked like and a brief history.

MOUNTFITCHET CASTLE STANSTED
OS 167   TL5225

In 1215 during the reign of John, soldiers were sent into Essex after a campaign in the north and west of England. Their aim was to destroy or capture any castle belonging to the rebel barons who had opposed the King.   Richard de Mountfitchet was one of many barons who were dissatisfied with the king's rule. Twenty five barons were present when King John had to agree to and seal the Magna Carta at Runnymede on 15 June 1215, and Richard de Mountfitchet was one of them. The barons, men of high rank and major land holders, were on the point of rebellion when the great charter was presented to the king. John was furious, soon after the event and, with the help of Pope Innocent III, annulment of the charter was declared. King John sent for troops from the continent, and the scene was set for civil war with the barons.

Soon castles in Essex were laid to siege, Hedingham and Colchester surrendered to the king's mercenaries, while other barons continued to campaign against John.   Richard de Mountfitchet now fled to his castle at Stansted to escape the king's wrath, the other barons retreated to their castles and estates around the county.

The castle at Stansted was built on a natural hill, probably on the site of ancient earthworks. A Saxon settlement may have already been established here when in 1066 William, after victory at Hastings, gave Robert Gernon, a Norman knight, many estates including Stansted as a reward for his loyalty.   The settlement consisted of two large circles of land in a figure of 8 with a wooden drawbridge connecting the two rings; this was called a ring and bailey. This was an older style of earthwork used before the conical earth mound (the motte), with its wooden tower and moated bailey that appeared soon after the conquest of 1066.   Robert Gernon built and strengthened his settlement here around the perimeter of the rings, placing high wooden stakes to enclose the land and form a stockade, with a gate to the outer bailey and a drawbridge inside to the inner ring, where he would live in relative safety with his family. He built kitchens and workshops along with stables and buildings for his soldiers, all done to make life tolerable in a hostile land. It was a time of great danger for the Normans, who could come under attack from the local Saxons at any time. As time went by life in the castle settled to a routine of daily tasks. The castle was almost a self contained unit. The residents were able to grow some food, but probably traded with the locals who would call at the castle to sell their surplus vegetables or exchange them for metal tools made by the castle's blacksmith. In the outer bailey animals would be kept for food: sheep for their meat and wool, cattle for meat and milk, geese, ducks and chickens for meat and eggs, bees for honey;

there was even a small fish pond. They were able to make and dye their own clothes and make their own tools and weapons.

Robert Gernon was lord of this community. He had reasonable accommodation in the inner bailey which could only be reached by crossing the wooden drawbridge guarded by Norman soldiers. Here was the great hall where the lord lived with his family; it was here that he would greet guests and important matters of the day were discussed. Meals and banquets were held here, the guests sat at long trestle tables that held the food and were waited on by the lord's servants.

This long room would be decorated with banners and shields hanging on the walls, and lit by candles and burning braziers. It was usual for music to be played while the meals were in progress, and after the meal the lord and his family would retire to the upstairs rooms for privacy and safety. The family would sleep undisturbed with a guard on the stairs. The great hall was the place where all important documents and money were held. These and the weapons were kept here under lock and key and the watchful eye of a guard. So this was the Normans' new way of life in England. They had won a great battle in 1066, now they had to win over the people and try to live with the Saxons who resented the Normans and their way of life. That is why the castle was built, to keep the locals in check, exploit the land and to help the Norman lord become rich on the spoils of battle.

Robert died and his son William inherited the castle. He did a strange thing by changing his surname from Gernon to Mountfitchet, and that is the name we know today as the place named Stansted Mountfichet. William enlarged and strengthened the castle with stone. The old wooden fences were pulled down and replaced with stone: this was called a curtain wall, a fragment can be seen today outside the reconstructed timber walls of the inner ring. There may have been projecting towers along the wall for the soldiers to look along the wall for intruders. General improvements were made to living facilities, and the buildings in the inner and outer bailey were strengthened and enlarged, the emphasis now on comfort and strength as Stansted was firmly established as a Norman stronghold.

William's son Gilbert continued the name Mountfitchet, and his son Richard was to become sheriff of Essex and keeper of the forests of Essex.

When he died in 1203 his son, also Richard, was only twelve years old. He inherited the estates and was put under the guidance of Roger de Lacy, a Norman knight. Richard grew up and by all accounts lived to become 'a most valiant knight', but now in 1215 he was confronted by King John and his soldiers who were about to attack his castle.

The walls were breached and the buildings set on fire. The castle was razed to the ground and Richard and his followers fled seeking shelter from other sympathetic barons.

A year later John died, and his son was crowned King Henry III in 1216. Richard was reinstated into royal favour, and his titles and lands were restored to him. Richard never married so there were no heirs; when he died in 1258 the estate was divided between his three sisters. One sister, Margaret, married Hugh de Bolebeck of Northumberland, who managed the estate, passing it to his heirs over the years. Eventually in 1334, the land became part of the De Vere family estate: they were the Earls of Oxford, and their family home was at Castle Hedingham.

The Mountfitchet name faded away like the castle, that was never rebuilt after it was destroyed by King John. The stone from the castle was carried off by the local villagers and used for building; the land was abandoned and overgrown.

Now 700 years later, the visitor can climb the hill and walk into the reconstructed settlement of the first Richard de Mountfitchet. What we see today is a ring and bailey on a hill; steps will take you to the gate of the bailey, that has a wooden palisade around its perimeter. Inside you will find reconstructed wattle and daub building that housed the workforce that served the Norman community. The inner ring is reached over a drawbridge; this is where the baron would live with his family in the great hall.

The visitor can step back in time and see and hear a reconstruction of the first lord at supper in the great hall. The whole setting of Stansted Castle has been thoroughly researched. Experts in ancient buildings and historians have made this place a mirror of life in the eleventh century.

The castle is open to visitors daily from spring to autumn, and there is an excellent souvenir guide on sale to help you understand the site. It is the only reconstructed ring and bailey castle you will find in Britain, and an experience you will find fascinating.

GREAT CANFIELD CASTLE
OS 167   TL 5918

Great Canfield is one of the places you need an Ordnance Survey map to find, hidden among the lanes and byways of the Roding villages. The name Canfield derives from the word *canes or reeds,* which grew in the marshy area by the river Roding, hence Canfield.

Turn off the Old Roman road leading from Leaden Roding to Dunmow at High Roding and wind your way through the lanes to the village of Great Canfield. Here you will find a thousand years of history. There is a collection of old cottages and houses, a Norman church and a motte and bailey type fortification.

The mound, 50 feet high and 280 feet across, can be found behind the church. This mound once had a great wooden tower on its summit, dominating the surrounding countryside. Inside the tower would be Norman soldiers armed with sword and shield, and in the bailey soldiers and horses ready to subdue the native Saxons if trouble arose

Several acres of the outer bailey still remain, where the community lived in the days after the Norman conquest. The site is now covered in trees and brambles, but the shape can clearly be seen from the top of the motte.

Little is known about the history of castle. Some say that Alberic de Vere owned it, along with his large estates at Castle Hedingham; others say that earthworks were here in Roman times.

25

Alberic de Vere came with Duke William of Normandy to fight on Senlac Hill, in 1066. Alberic was given lands taken from the defeated Saxons in Essex and Suffolk. It is probable that Canfield castle was raised at this time in the Norman style; quickly built and occupied, later abandoned for more substantial buildings at Hedingham, where the de Vere family established a lasting dynasty.

What we see today is a tree covered mound, water-filled ditches and earth banks. The land is flat in this area and you may not see the motte and bailey at first as it looks like a small wood or copse especially in summer. On a bleak winter's day it is more easily recognised when all the trees have lost their leaves, and the distinctive shape of the motte can be seen.

Use your imagination to see the castle and its occupants, picture Norman village life, the wooden tower on the mound, and the hustle and bustle inside the bailey behind its huge earth bank and wooden palisade. Smell the smoke from the fires, and the warm animal scents from the horses and cattle, hear the barking dogs and the clanging of the blacksmith's hammer.

A visit to the nearby church of St Mary's will be a pleasant surprise, it is a fine example of a Norman church with a 15th century spire. There are some interesting Norman stone carvings around the church. In the present day entrance you will see on one of the capitals (the head or top part of a column) a stone carving of a bearded man and two birds with long beaks either side of the head with their tails in the air. On another column a design of ancient origin appears in the form of a cross with four equal arms, each bent in a right angle. The design looks like a swastika, the emblem used by another country in modern times, who also had designs on conquering Britain as the Normans had done 800 years ago.

Inside the church a large chancel arch frames two small windows and a large mediæval painting of the Virgin Mary and the baby Jesus. It is 13th century in origin and still has its colours, red and yellow. Although faded over the years it is still a striking painting full of gentleness. The picture of a mother and her child has been admired for over 700 years, probably by the inhabitants of the castle, who would have attended the church as all good Christians, even in those violent days of Norman occupation. The church is now quietly mellowing in its peaceful surroundings.

Occasionally the sound of the church bell rings out from the bell tower and floats gently around the overgrown bailey, empty now except for the rooks and the rabbits who live where Norman knights once lived, it is easy to lose yourself in the past in this quietly evocative place.

PLESHEY CASTLE
OS 167   TL 6715

Shakespeare wrote of Pleshey, these words spoken by the Duchess Eleanor, widow of the murdered Duke of Gloucester to John of Gaunt,

> With all good speed at Pleshy visit me.
> Alack, and what shall good old York there see
> But empty lodgings and unfurnished walls,
> Unpeopled offices, untrodden stones.
> And what hear there for welcome but my groans. (*Richard II,* Act
1 Scene 2)

Richard II, King of England 1377-1413, had put to death his uncle, Thomas of Woodstock, Earl of Buckingham and Duke of Gloucester in 1397, Eleanor was contemplating her fate living at Pleshey without her husband because the king had seized the castle and estate for himself. Gloucester's death was brought about as a result of the king's determination for revenge after he had to endure years of humiliation, his authority to rule constantly undermined by his uncle the Duke of Gloucester. Richard was a minor aged 11 when he ascended the throne in 1377. He was the son of the Black Prince, who would have been king, but he died before his father, Edward III. Edward's other sons, Lionel of Antwerp, (Duke of Clarence,) John of Gaunt (Duke of Lancaster), Edmund of Langley (Duke of York) and Thomas of Woodstock (Duke of Gloucester), resented their young nephew and were to create problems for him when he became King. The story is full of plots and murder that would have far reaching implications that carried on for several decades, long after King Richard was dead. Gloucester soon established himself at the head of a group called the Lords Appellant.

This group were powerful men accusing Richard's friends of treason, and used Parliament to have them executed. This was called the 'merciless parliament' due to the severity of the sentences imposed on the accused

Apart from the Duke of Gloucester, the others were Richard Fitzalan, (Earl of Arundel), Thomas Beauchamp (Earl of Warwick), Henry Bolingbroke, (Earl of Derby), and Thomas Mowbray (Earl of Nottingham). They were all ambitious and ruthless, dictating policies to the king, even making appointments, yet the king was powerless to stop them. Gloucester was accumulating great wealth in the process.

The Duke was living at Pleshey castle with his wife Eleanor de Bohun who brought the castle when she married him. They lived in great splendour. An inventory taken after the Duke's death found among the many items recorded, a great bed of gold, costly tapestries and many rich linens and silks; these were just some of the items that the Duke had accumulated while he was in power.

He also founded a collegiate church at Pleshey to the south of the present church; it was a large and magnificent building for three priests, two clerks and two choristers. The Duke's power over the King was so great that he was excluding him from any decision making and isolating Richard from his friends, leaving the young king frustrated at his inability to rule. Richard bided his time, and when he was 23 declared his intent to rule without his uncles' help. King Richard's Queen, Ann of Bohemia, died in 1384, her death causing him much grief at the time, and it may have affected his mind. He now married Isabella, daughter of Charles VI of France, as a diplomatic gesture; she was only seven years old at the time, but it brought peace with France after many years of war.

The country accepted the king's rule, but Richard harboured thoughts of revenge towards his uncle and the Lords Appellant for the injustice and humiliation he had endured as a boy king. An uneasy peace settled over the country.

Then in 1397 Richard arrived unexpectedly with his followers at the gates of Pleshey Castle. His uncle, the Duke of Gloucester, was in residence and alarmed by the sudden appearance of the king, who insisted that his uncle accompany him to London for a meeting of King's council. Horses were saddled and made ready for the journey to London.

Richard and Gloucester set out from Pleshey riding together at first, but as the journey progressed the king went ahead with his escort and Gloucester was kept at the rear. When the party reached Stratford-atte-Bow, the Earl Marshal, Thomas Mowbray, rode up to Gloucester and arrested him for treason. He cried out to the king to save him, but Richard ignored his pleas and rode on to London. Gloucester was whisked on board a ship in the Thames, to set sail for Calais. When the ship arrived in France the Earl Marshal and his prisoner went into Calais Castle, where the Duke started to contemplate his fate. A few days later he was moved to a local inn, where he anxiously awaited news from England.

One evening that September while the Duke was preparing for dinner, four men rushed into the room, threw towels around his neck and strangled him. The Earl Marshal put him on the bed and declared the Duke of Gloucester dead; later King Richard was informed that his uncle had died of a heart attack! The Duke's body was brought back to England, resting at Hadleigh Castle before proceeding to Pleshey, where he was buried in his own collegiate church, later the body was moved to Westminster Abbey. The Duchess Eleanor was broken hearted over the death of her husband, retreating to a nunnery at Barking, eventually returning to Pleshey where she died in October 1399. King Richard took possession of the Duke's castle and lands at Pleshey for himself, even placing a plaque over the castle's gateway with the words RICARDUS REX II, declaring that this was now his property and that his uncle was dead. This plaque can now be seen in the choir vestry in Holy Trinity Church, Pleshey. King Richard then had the other members of the Appellants arrested. The Earl of Arundel was beheaded in the Tower of London, and the Earl of Warwick sent to prison; the others either fled the country or were banished by the King.

The plaque in
The choir vestry
in Holy Trinity
Church, Pleshey

This action by the King caused great alarm in Parliament and among the other barons, as his behaviour was becoming more and more erratic. Then in 1399, John of Gaunt died and Richard seized and confiscated his uncle's great estates, an act that would eventually lead to his downfall. Henry Bolingbroke (John of Gaunt's son) had been exiled by King Richard when the Appellants had been disbanded, and was living in France. He was entitled to his father's estates, and made preparations to come to England with an army to claim his inheritance. King Richard was in Ireland when Bolingbroke landed in Yorkshire, where many supporters joined him, tired of the king's conduct and tyrannical rule.

Richard returned to England to find that he had lost the trust and support of Parliament and the people and was eventually forced to abdicate. Richard was imprisoned in Pontefract Castle, where he later died. A story was circulated that Richard had starved himself to death, but he was probably murdered as he would be a threat while he lived, even in captivity, to the new order and the new king. Henry Bolingbroke was now accepted as ruler and was crowned Henry IV in 1399. His claim to the throne was validated as he was Richard's cousin and the grandson of Edward III.

After Richard's death, his followers fled the court in fear for their lives. The Duke of Exeter, Richard's half-brother, who was responsible for conspiring in the capture of the Duke of Gloucester, was making his escape from London when he fell into the hands of the late duke's men. He was taken to Pleshey Castle under guard where, in revenge for the death of their master, the Duke of Gloucester, they cut off his head in the bailey yard, then placed it on a pole and displayed it on the castle walls. Richard's reign was over, Henry IV was king, and Pleshey Castle fell silent.

The Duke of Gloucester and his wife Eleanor were dead and their retainers gone, the fine ornaments and furniture taken from the castle, the rooms were empty and cold awaiting a new tenant.

This was not the first time that Pleshey had seen drama around its earth ramparts and walls. The origins of the castle are not clear; Roman remains have been found in the area, and the Saxons called the place Tumbleton which means small hill or ancient place.

A Saxon village grew up around the old earthworks, enclosing itself with earth banks and waterfilled ditches. After the conquest by the Normans in 1066 the name Pleshey appears, which is an old French word meaning enclosure. The village and other estates in the surrounding area were given to a Norman knight, Geoffrey de Mandeville, as a reward for his loyalty and service to William, Duke of Normandy, at the great battle. It was probably then, that the motte was raised and a wooden castle and palisade built, as was the fashion of the Normans soon after the conquest. It was another Geoffrey de Mandeville, grandson of the first Norman owner, who, in the reign of Stephen (1135-54), strengthened the motte, and raised it to 55 feet and over 250 feet in diameter.

He built earth ramparts and had a deep water-filled moat dug around part of the motte and the inner bailey. Geoffrey pulled down the old wooden keep on the mound, and built substantial buildings of stone, both as a home for himself, and as a defensive castle; the whole area, including the outer town enclosure, covered over 40 acres. Geoffrey de Mandeville was the son of William de Mandeville and succeeded to his father's title as Constable of the Tower of London. In the civil war that raged between King Stephen and Empress Matilda over the crown of England, Geoffrey was able to play one against the other for financial rewards and power. He first supported the King, obtaining the title Earl of Essex, gaining several estates and land for a castle he later built at Walden.

In 1141 he met Matilda in London and took her side in the conflict to obtain further titles for himself. He became Sheriff of Essex with all the privileges and the extra revenue the post offered, adding to the great wealth and power he already had. Later he switched sides again, deserting Matilda when London would not accept her as queen, after Stephen was defeated in a battle and captured at Lincoln. The King was later released and Matilda fled the country.

Geoffrey's terms for his loyalty went high; a pardon for supporting Matilda, and further grants of lands and titles including Sheriff of London and Middlesex, which the King gave reluctantly. Geoffrey de Mandeville was now one of the most powerful men in the country. He held the title Earl of Essex, was Sheriff of three counties, Constable of the Tower of London, the owner of many estates in Essex along with two castles, Pleshey and Walden. Even the King now felt threatened by Geoffrey's power, with good cause as he was having secret meetings with Matilda, who was planning to continue her fight for the throne of

England. Geoffrey's demands on Matilda's generosity were great, extracting from her more privileges and honours to add to his already vast wealth. The king meanwhile was kept informed of Geoffrey's movements, intending to curb his power when the opportunity arose.

This came when Matilda's bid for the throne failed and her cause lost. Geoffrey was accused of treason and forced to surrender his castles at Pleshey and Walden, he also lost his titles and the Tower of London, the real power behind his authority and ambitions. He fled London under the threat of death from the king, with all the rage and fury of a man in torment. His immediate plan was to seek help from powerful friends. He then quickly established himself in the fens of Cambridgeshire, hiding like an outlaw with his band of followers, sallying forth looting and pillaging churches and the surrounding area.

The tomb of Geofffrey de Mandeville in the Temple Church

The king sent soldiers into the fens after Geoffrey, but the terrain was too difficult to penetrate. Geoffrey's defeat came when he attacked an outpost and was wounded in the head, later dying from his injuries in 1144. For his crimes against the church he was excommunicated and denied a church burial. For many years his body laid unburied in a lead coffin at Temple Church in London until his son appealed to the Pope for absolution for his father, finally granted twenty years after his father's death. A stone effigy lies on the floor of Temple Church to this day, supposedly that of Geoffrey himself. Under Henry II the estates and castles at Pleshey and Walden were restored to Geoffrey de Mandeville's son, also named Geoffrey, who kept building and adding to the castles and estates for many years. Henry gave permission to Geoffrey's son, William de Mandeville, the third Earl, to completely re-strengthen the earthworks and to fortify his castle at Pleshey. He went on a crusade joining the Knights Templar at Jerusalem, later returning to England in 1178 with the spoils of war.

In 1180 William married Havice, the daughter of the Count of Aumale, whose family were also wealthy land owners. Now with his titles, castles and large estates enhanced by his marriage, the de Mandevilles were once again a powerful force in England. Henry II sent William de Mandeville to France as his representative on many occasions as diplomat and courier as well as a soldier, when problems arose over Henry's French held territories. William remained loyal to the king until Henry's death in 1189. A new King was crowned and William had the honour of carrying the crown at the coronation of Richard I.

That same year 1189, William died in Rouen, Normandy; he had no children to inherit his titles. His widow Havice later married William de Fortibus, who acquired the earldom of Aumale. The English estates went initially to Beatrice de Mandeville, sister of the first Earl, and then to her daughter Beatrice, who married Geoffrey FitzPiers. He supported Prince John through his troubled regency in England while his brother King Richard I was out of the country. Richard died in 1199 and John became King. For his loyalty to John, Geoffrey was rewarded with the title fourth Earl of Essex; his other titles included Sheriff of Essex and Hertfordshire and Chief Justice of England. He died in 1213 leaving his son, also Geoffrey, to become the fifth Earl, later changing the family name from FitzPiers to de Mandeville. Geoffrey did not have the same loyalty to King John as his father had. He married the King's ex-wife, Isabella of Gloucester, and received the title Earl of Gloucester, paying the King handsomely for the privilege. He opposed the king over the terms of Magna Carta in 1215 and became one of the rebel barons, retreating to his castle at Pleshey when King John went on the rampage throughout the country, exacting revenge on all who had opposed him. The castle survived John's onslaught but the adjacent village suffered at the hands of the king's French mercenaries.

Peace resumed later that year when King John died and his son Henry was crowned king. Geoffrey died a year later when he was injured in a tournament. He was succeeded by his brother William, who became the sixth Earl of Essex. William held the estates until he died in 1227, when his sister Maud, who had married Henry de Bohun, inherited the castle and estates; she therefore became the Countess of Essex.

After her death in 1236 the title Earl of Essex went to the de Bohun family and continued for several generations until the twelfth Earl, who died in 1360. The estates and castles went to his nephew Humphrey along with the title Earl and High Constable of England. He had two daughters, Eleanor and Mary. Both girls married into influential families

Mary, the youngest daughter, married Henry Bolingbroke, the son of John of Gaunt. Bolingbroke was later to become King Henry IV; Mary bore him four sons, the eldest to reign as King Henry V, and two daughters. Mary died in 1394 before Henry became king. Eleanor de Bohun the eldest daughter, married Thomas of Woodstock, who later became the Duke of Gloucester, whose story is told at the start of this chapter.

The fall of the Duke marked the end of the de Mandeville and de Bohun families' influence over the land; the castle at Pleshey was abandoned and empty, and the collegiate church had lost its patron, but not for long. After Eleanor's death in 1399 her elderly mother, the Countess of Hertfordshire, lived at the castle for a short while. On her death the castle and estates went to the Duke of Gloucester's daughter Ann, the wife of Edmund, the fifth Earl of Stafford. The Stafford family were loyal to the Lancaster dynasty.

In 1403 Edmund was killed at the battle of Shrewsbury defending King Henry IV against the Percy family, powerful landowners from the north of England, who had a grievance against the king. After the Earl's death problems arose over his estates, even the king claiming Pleshey Castle for himself as part of the estates of his first wife Mary de Bohun. A legal wrangle was to continue for many years until Henry V requisitioned the estates into the Duchy of Lancaster. After Earl Stafford's death, his son Humphrey, who was only one year old when he inherited his father's estates, including Pleshey, later became the sixth Earl. Little is known about his early life, but when he was 20 years old he was knighted by Henry V for his service in France.

King Henry died in 1422 soon after his son was born, facing an uncertain future as King Henry VI in the hands of his uncles, John of Lancaster and Humphrey, Duke of Gloucester. Henry grew up to become pious and scholarly, not a strong ruler, more interested in philosophy than politics. He married Margaret of Anjou. She was a strong willed woman, who would stop at nothing to protect her husband against the powerful earls and dukes in the kingdom, especially the Duke of York whom the queen hated. Richard, Duke of York, was recognised as successor if the king died without an heir, as both families claimed royal descent from Edward III. King Henry VI was subject to fits of madness, an illness that plagued him through his troubled reign. A son was born to Queen Margaret and Henry, but the king was too ill to recognise his son Edward, even when presented to him. Eventually Margaret nursed him back to health, but the King was never strong.

Humphrey, Earl of Stafford's loyalty to the king was to bring rich rewards for himself and his wife Ann, daughter of Ralph Neville, first Earl of Westmorland.

He was made a Knight of the Garter, and later became the Earl of Buckingham after his mother Ann died in 1438. Two years later he became the first Duke of Buckingham. He stayed loyal to the Lancastrian cause, as quarrelling between the nobles who surrounded the king developed into open rebellion and then civil war.

This eventually led to war between the houses of York and Lancaster (supporters of the king) known later as the Wars of the Roses; the year was 1455. The first conflict was at St Albans. Humphrey, Duke of Buckingham, allied himself with Queen Margaret and the Lancastrian cause. He was wounded in the face while engaged in battle; then retreated to his estate to recover. Queen Margaret was a frequent visitor to Pleshey Castle, and it was probably about this time that the great brick bridge was built. The bridge spans the bailey across the moat to the top of the motte. The single arch 18 feet high 18 feet wide has been described as unique and may be the oldest brickbuilt bridge in Europe.

The war raged on. Humphrey was eventually killed while leading the left flank for the King against Warwick 'the king maker' on 10th July 1460 at

Northampton. He died a wealthy man, one of the great landowners of England; money was left to the college and church at Pleshey, where his remains were buried. Today his tombstone hangs on the wall in Holy Trinity Church; the stone is in poor condition but you can see the outline of the missing brasses of Humphrey and his wife. The dynastic war between the houses of York and Lancaster continued.

At the battle of Tewkesbury in 1471 the king's son, Prince Edward of Lancaster, was killed and the king put into the Tower of London by Edward, the son of the Duke of York. Queen Margaret fled the country and went to France. The king later died in the Tower, probably murdered. The new king was now the Yorkist Edward IV, crowned in Westminster Abbey in 1461 at 19 years of age.

The Staffords continued to remain a family of wealth and influence with their titles and estates. The title second Duke of Buckingham went to Humphrey's grandson Henry, who rose to prominence in the reign of Richard III. He assisted the then Duke of Gloucester (Richard) in the arrest of Lord Rivers and Lord Gray, who were escorting the young Prince Edward to London after his father the king had died. Later the prince and his brother were sent to the Tower, never to be seen again and probably murdered on the Duke of Buckingham's orders. Richard rewarded him for his services with many titles, including Lord High Constable and Chief Justice, and all the royal estates in Wales, including the castles; this made him a very wealthy man. Richard was offered the crown of England, but was slow to accept at first. He requested Buckingham to speak to the citizens of London on his behalf and to judge if he would be accepted as king by the people. Richard promised that when he became king he would make Buckingham heir to the de Bohun family estates which had come to the crown from Henry V.

Richard was crowned king in 1483 and Buckingham carried the monarch's train and was rewarded with some of the old Duchy of Lancaster's estates.

Later that year Henry Stafford, Duke of Buckingham, for so long a friend and ally of Richard, turned against the king intending to replace him with Henry Tudor, a contender for the throne. Buckingham fled to Shropshire to escape Richard's wrath. He went into hiding only to be betrayed to Richard's soldiers and was taken to Salisbury where he was executed in the town square. All his estates were forfeited to the crown . Later Richard was killed at Bosworth and Henry Tudor then reigned as King Henry VII.

Henry Stafford's son Edward became the third Duke of Buckingham, serving the new king and was made a Knight of the Garter in 1495. In 1509 on the accession of Henry VIII, Edward became Lord High Constable and the king's steward. He carried the crown at Henry's coronation and later became Captain of the English army in France. Although high in the King's favour, suspicions over Buckingham's past relatives making trouble for the crown were always in King

Henry's mind. This gave Edward's enemies ammunition with which to discredit him. Buckingham quarrelled with Cardinal Wolsey and others in the court, which led to trumped-up charges of treason. Buckingham was arrested and put into the Tower of London awaiting trial. In 1521 he was condemned to death and beheaded on Tower Hill. The death of Edward Stafford, Duke of Buckingham, also heralded the end of the title High Constable of England, as the office was abolished by Henry VIII in 1521.

Pleshey Castle had been the official residence of the High Constable; now its important rôle had gone it started to deteriorate very quickly. A reference to the bridge in the year 1589 described it as 'the olde arche of bryckework', so must have been ancient then.

After the great days of Eleanor and Thomas Woodstock, the castle went into decline. It became part of the Duchy of Lancaster and any revenue from the castle went straight to the crown; very little was given back for repairs. In 1540 the dissolution of the monasteries was completed in England after Henry VIII declared himself head of the English church and broke away from the church of Rome. In 1546 the collegiate church at Pleshey surrendered to the crown. The altar plate and vestments were sold off and the priests dismissed from their posts. Soon the buildings were abandoned and suffering from neglect. King Henry gave some Essex estates, including the castle and church at Pleshey, to Sir John Gates as a reward for his service to the King.

Sir John was a member of Henry VIII's Privy Council and Justice of the Peace for the county of Essex. He immediately started to demolish the chancel of the church, selling the stone to the locals as building materials, much to the dismay of the parishioners who pleaded with him to stop the destruction. Broken tombstones from the church lay scattered about including that of John Holland, Earl of Exeter, the half brother to Richard III, who was executed at Pleshey.

The people of Pleshey raised some money to purchase the bells and steeple and the shell of the church, but the damage had been done. In time the church was rebuilt, but the castle lost its buildings, the stone being sold locally, leaving the grass motte and bailey that we see today.

Henry VIII died in 1547 and his young son reigned as Edward VI, but at the age of 15 years he was suffering from consumption, and not expected to live very long. One of the most powerful men in the country was the Duke of Northumberland who was plotting with other leading magnates including Sir John Gates to place Lady Jane Gray on the throne when the young king died. The reason was to keep the Catholic Mary, daughter of Henry VIII and Catherine of Aragon, off the throne, and to keep the Protestant faith in England. But the conspiracy was discovered and Sir John Gates arrested; Northumberland quickly deserted Sir John and supported Mary. The parishioners of Pleshey must have gained some satisfaction when Sir John Gates was brought to trial, found guilty for his part in the conspiracy, and beheaded on Tower Hill.

Northumberland met a similar fate later. All of Sir John Gates' lands and property were confiscated by the crown. The young King Edward died and Mary was crowned queen 30th November 1553.

This was the end of Pleshey, the home of powerful men. Gone are the de Mandevilles, de Bohuns and Staffords. This was not a happy place for these great men and their descendants. The list of tragic events that followed these families through the centuries makes fearful reading;

Geoffrey de Mandeville, renegade and outlaw killed in a skirmish 1144

The Duke of Gloucester murdered 1397

The Duchess Eleanor died of a broken heart soon after 1399

The Duke of Exeter, half brother to Richard II, beheaded at Pleshey

Mary de Bohun died young in childbirth she might have been Queen had she lived

Edmund Stafford, fifth Earl of Stafford, killed at the battle of Shrewsbury 1403

Humphrey Stafford, first Duke of Buckingham, killed at the battle of Northampton 1460

Henry Stafford, second Duke of Buckingham, beheaded for treason by Richard II 1483

Edward Stafford, third Duke of Buckingham, beheaded for treason by Henry VIII 1521

Sir John Gates executed for supporting Lady Jane Gray 1553

Pleshey is one of the best preserved motte and bailey earthworks you will see anywhere in the country. The village was established at the same time as the castle and is still contained in the original outer town enclosure.

Pleshey is 8 miles north west of Chelmsford, between the villages of High Easter and Great Waltham. The castle is privately owned and is protected by law through the Ancient Monuments and Archæological Areas Act 1979.

There is a telephone number if you wish to visit the castle on a display board in a viewing area that is open to the public. You have to phone for an appointment to view the motte and bailey at close hand. A small fee is payable; in return you get the keys to the bailey gate and a short guide to the castle.

Walk over the brick bridge to the top of the motte to see the village below, tucked around the outer enclosure. Then look forward into the empty bailey, where the buildings and houses that supported the castle once stood. It does not take much imagination to see the castle at work: the people milling about, the noises of the crowd, the sound of hammers on metal from the blacksmith's shop, dogs barking, horses and riders arriving at the drawbridge, soldiers in the tavern. Then suddenly a jumbo jet roars overhead and you come back to the twenty-first century.

CLAVERING CASTLE
OS 167   TL 4732

Imagination must play a part when you visit Clavering, for all that is left of this important castle are earthworks, a series of undulating bumps of grass covered earth over an acre of ground.

There are no ruins of a great castle, just flat ground and earth ramparts surrounding the site, with the remains of a water filled moat and steep earth banks over 50 feet wide. A complex system of earthworks near the river shows that the site had a watermill, with sluices in the earthworks to control the water flow to and from the moat for the mill. This would indicate that the castle was well designed and self-sufficient. Nothing remains of the substantial stone castle that once stood here, masonry from the buildings has long gone, but this is an historic place. A household once flourished here, the owner was a Norman and friend of King Edward the Confessor.

The site lies north of the present church of St Mary and St Clement. A footpath will lead you to the edge of the south rampart, then around the west side of the rectangular earthworks. The river Stort, from its humble beginnings as a small stream, meanders around the north side of the moat, which is much overgrown with trees and shrubs, and then heads towards Bishop's Stortford.

There is no contemporary picture of what the castle may have looked like, but it is safe to assume that it is one of the earliest Norman castles in Essex, built as a fortified home, possibly in the style depicted on the Bayeux tapestry.

Harold at Bosham

In an early scene from the tapestry, Harold is seen in his manor house feasting at Bosham in Sussex. The building has arched pillars, an outside stairway leading to an upper room, and a tiled roof. The house is, of course, stylized for the tapestry, but it shows that the building was constructed in stone and could hold a large number of people.

The Normans had been building castles in France for many years both for defence and as fortified homes, but the Saxons had no need to build such structures. England had been at peace for many years; the raiding parties from the bad old days were gone, when the Danes were rampaging through the countryside. They had settled down, married English girls, and become farmers; old enemies of the past had integrated into the community, and there was no need for massive stone keeps, unlike their continental neighbours. There was very little need for the people to defend themselves from invaders, only from thieves and wild beasts from the forest.

Surrounding the settlements were earth banks and ditches, usually to stop the cattle from straying, and the villa houses snuggled together surrounded by thick forests, sheltering the people from the troubles of the outside world. The young men practiced with staff and bow, and the villagers went about their daily business, their lives governed by the agricultural year and the Christian faith.

Robert Fitz-Wymarc, a Norman who had been living in England for many years, had acquired extensive lands in Essex, and was the King's 'Staller' or Steward and Horse Master at the king's palace, as well as being Edward's friend and confidant. He had come to England from Normandy with Edward along with other nobles, architects and craftsmen and was granted lands in Essex for his services to the king: land at Rayleigh was the seat of the king's hereditary standard bearer, which was one of Robert's duties. Robert's son, Swein, developed Rayleigh into a fortified castle after 1066.

Robert Fitz-Wymarc was granted permission by Edward the Confessor to build his castle or fortified house at Clavering probably between 1042 and 1048, and this enabled him to live in comfort and entertain his Norman friends. It also provided some degree of safety as, although he was anglicised, he was still a Norman and treated with suspicion by the locals, but appears to have been trusted by the English nobility. It was not unusual for fortified houses to be built in Edward's reign; the existing Saxon nobility had no reason to be worried about such buildings, as they posed no threat to anybody prior to 1066.

He went to see Duke William of Normandy who had landed in Sussex with a great army with the intent of giving battle to King Harold for the English crown. Robert tried to persuade William to abandon this risky venture as Harold was a formidable force. He had just defeated the Vikings at Stamford Bridge even killing his own brother Tostig and was at this very moment heading towards William with an elated army.

William's response was inevitable, that he was not concerned about Harold and his army; he had come to claim the throne he believed was his, a promise made to him by his cousin King Edward and Harold had sworn an oath while William's guest to support his claim

To William, Harold was an oath breaker, and this was a holy crusade, he even had a papal banner given to him by Pope Alexander. Robert Fitz-Wymarc then left William returning to London, and then to his home in Essex.

After William's victory at Hastings and the death of King Harold, Robert was allowed to keep his castles and lands in Essex, probably because he was of Norman origin and a friend of the late King Edward; it appears that William did not hold any grudge against Robert for defending Harold.

Clavering Castle remained the home of Robert until his death. Then his son Swein inherited his father's estates and titles, including sheriff of Essex, and all the lands and castle at Rayleigh where Swein went to live, leaving the old family home at Clavering.

Little is known about the fate of the castle; it may have been confiscated in the wars of Stephen and Matilda from 1135-54 or destroyed by King John when he was on the rampage in Essex in 1215. Today it is a tangle of shrubs and grass, somewhere to walk the dog - the bricks and mortar have gone but the history remains forever in our minds.

HEDINGHAM CASTLE
OS 155   TL 7936

The village of Castle Hedingham lies off the A604 between Colchester and Haverhill. The name Hedingham is a old Saxon word and means 'village or inhabitants at the head of a pasture'. It is the only town in Essex to have a castle incorporated into its name. The castle dominates the village and can be seen towering above the trees. A formidable sight today, consider how it appeared to the poor Saxon who saw this great building raised by the foreign invader to curtail his freedom.

The origins of the castle, and the beginnings of a great family dynasty began when Alberic de Vere, a Norman knight, was given estates in Essex. These were taken from Wulfwine, a Saxon landowner, who had supported King Harold at the great battle in Sussex when the Normans arrived. Alberic de Vere came from Normandy as the Lord of Ver, a town near Bayeux. Apart from the lands in Essex, he received estates in Suffolk, Cambridgeshire and Middlesex from William (now king of England).

Alberic made his home at Hedingham, marrying a Norman noblewoman named Beatrice. Over the years he raised his family and, despite his many duties to King William, found time to plant a vineyard at Hedingham and founded a Priory at Colne, later called Earls Colne. The great stone castle keep that we see today was not built until Alberic died; his son, Alberic II, had the castle constructed between 1130 and 1140. He probably used the same plans that the architect, and later Archbishop of Canterbury, William de Corbeuil, used in 1127 for Rochester Castle in Kent because they look very similar in design and were built about the same time. Hedingham, the larger and finer, was built using ashlar stone as a facing.

The castle is very strongly built; the great keep is 100 feet high and nearly 60 feet wide with walls 12 feet thick at the base and a square turret in each corner, two of them rising above the top of the keep. It stands on a semi-natural mound in the inner bailey, with a large outer bailey to the east of the castle.

Between the inner and outer walls of the castle, flint and stone rubble were mixed with mortar for strength. The facing stones on the outer walls were from quarries in Northamptonshire and were brought to Hedingham overland, an expensive undertaking for the de Veres, but no expense was spared for this symbol of Norman might. Other buildings were constructed around the great tower in the inner bailey in Tudor times. These are now gone leaving only the great keep and a Tudor brick bridge crossing the dry moat constructed in 1496 by John, 13th Earl of Oxford. To the west of the castle the entrance to the keep was up a stone staircase through the forebuilding, a building built on to the side of the keep and over the stairs to protect the entrance against attack. This led to a large arched entrance decorated with the familiar chevron or zig-zag pattern much favoured by the Normans. There was also a portcullis that could be lowered down over the entrance, operated from the room above. Through the doorway and into the keep was the first floor. You would have been met by the castle's soldiers who were on duty that day wearing conical helmets and chain mail hauberk (coat of steel), leather belt and sword, kite-shaped shield, and spear, for this was the guard room or the garrison. It was here that the castle guards lived. They would cook their meals, sleep when not on duty, clean and maintain their weapons. There is a large fireplace in this room with an arch in the usual zig-zag pattern. With a little imagination you can see the soldiers sitting around the fire at night to keep warm, gambling and grumbling about their problems until the dawn, when the fires were stoked up ready for the day ahead. The windows in the garrison were very narrow so that the soldiers could look out and fire their arrows at an enemy with few missiles, arrows, stones, etc, reaching inside the castle from an attack outside. In this room was a small lavatory for the household's use.

The next floor was reached by a large spiral staircase 13 feet wide, it also went down to the ground floor to the storage area. This is where the food was stored; the walls were the thickest here, no windows just narrow slits so that hardly any daylight came in, and just enough air to keep the food cool. Stored here would be provisions for a large household, flour, salted meat, rabbits and hares when available, ale and wine. Not many vegetables were eaten; when they were it was mostly cabbage and onions, and these mainly used in soups and stew. Nuts and fruit were used when in season. Herbs and spices were used regularly for health and flavour; the spices would probably be kept under lock and key as they were very scarce and expensive to buy. Fish and eels from the rivers and lakes were brought in, salted, then stored for later use. Chickens and geese would wander into the bailey; they too would find their way to the Norman lord's table.

Cattle and goats were kept for meat, milk and cheese; sometimes bees were kept for honey used to sweeten puddings and drinks. The inhabitants of the castle ate very well with food in plentiful supply, whereas the country people had a limited dict of coarse bread, milk, eggs and cheese; meat was only available on special occasions. The horses from the castle would be stabled in the inner bailey for safety. Fodder for the animals may have been stored in the basement area in bad weather and in times of siege, but this item would be rather too bulky and smelly to stay for long in the castle. Water was usually freely available from the well in the basement, and rainwater could be collected and stored in wooden tanks inside the castle.

At Hedingham the kitchens were situated in separate buildings in the inner bailey, near the castle walls. Kitchens had been separated in the past when castles were made of timber, because of fear of fire. The household were probably used to eating food that was not piping hot, as it had to be carried across the castle yard, and up several flights of stairs to the grand hall.

Returning to the staircase above the first floor (the garrison) the second floor held the great hall or banqueting room, where Lord de Vere would hold court and conduct the business of the day. It was also used for meals and entertaining guests. The Norman lord and his lady would dine here at the head of a large table with the rest of guests or household at tables around the room. Musicians would play in the gallery that runs around the entire room, high above the floor so they could look down on the activities below. Fires would be burning in the large fireplaces, candles would be lighted around the room, shields with the coat of arms of the de Veres (a five pointed star), and coloured banners would be hanging on the walls. Servants brought food to the tables, and dogs roamed around looking for scraps of food, sometimes fighting over a discarded bone. The scene would be full of movement and noise with people talking and laughing. Sometimes acrobats and travelling players would entertain the diners, so that meals were a great social event and could last many hours. Towering above the people in this room is a great stone arch, the largest Norman arch in Europe, 28 feet wide and 20 feet high supported on pillars either side of the room. The fireplaces and some of the windows, which are larger here than the lower rooms, are richly decorated with the usual zigzag or chevron design making this one of most delightful of rooms in the castle and one of the best examples of Norman workmanship you will find anywhere in England. Above the banqueting hall, continuing up the spiral staircase you will find the solar, an upper room for sleeping and a private room for the Lord and Lady of the castle and their guards. Here was a fireplace for comfort; the ladies would work their tapestries and gossip about the day. They would then retire to sleep in wooden beds with wool or linen blankets. The guards would stand outside the doors and some would sleep rolled in their cloaks on the floor.

Alberic II was a very busy man - hunting wild boar and hawking, administering the estates, making money, and seeing to affairs of state kept him occupied most of the day. This then was life soon after the castle was built in the 12th century. It was mainly built to defend the household from an enemy attack or a siege that might last for many months, and its secondary purpose was a home for the knight and his retinue. A castle on this grand scale was pure Norman, nothing like it existed in Britain before the Conquest; it was a statement by the invader that they had arrived and were intending to stay. As time went by, the rich estate and castle owners wanted more comfort. Clothes and furniture came from abroad. They became more sophisticated and stopped living in the cold keep, moving into more luxurious surroundings in the inner and outer bailey in purpose built houses. The keep remained for defensive purposes and as the centre for the administration of the great estate by a steward or overseer.

The de Vere family as the Earls of Oxford were in Essex for 20 generations and produced many famous and infamous men, soldiers of fortune, statesmen, politicians and churchmen. There are so many eminent men that it would take a whole book to write of their exploits, so a summary of the main characters and events is written here.

In 1133 Alberic II (1090-1141) was the master at Hedingham; he attended the king's court and was made Great Lord Chamberlain by Henry I. Later he was prominent in the court of King Stephen (1135-54). Alberic married Alice, the daughter of Gilbert FitzRichard, and had four sons and several daughters. One of them, Rohese, married Geoffrey de Mandeville

In 1135 Alberic founded a monastery at Hatfield Broad Oak on the site of the present day church of St Mary the Virgin and built the great castle keep at Hedingham which we see today, still standing after 800 years. Alberic was to die in London caught up in a riot in the city; his body was buried in his father's priory at Colne in Essex. His wife Alice lived for another twenty-two years withdrawing from society to live in St Osyth's Priory in Essex.

Alberic's son Aubrey III supported the Empress Maud (or Matilda), daughter of Henry I, in her bid for the throne when the King died in 1135. Her cousin Stephen had had himself crowned King while Maud was out of England. This led to civil war in which both sides had losses and gains and many lives were lost. In 1142 Aubrey was made Earl of Oxford by Empress Maud for his help and support in those difficult times. The title was later endorsed by Maud's son Henry when he was crowned Henry II after Stephen died in 1154. Stephen's wife Matilda had died two years earlier at Hedingham castle. Maud had not been accepted by the barons in London as queen, and fled to the continent where in 1164 she died in Normandy and is buried in Rouen Cathedral.

Aubrey III, the 1st Earl of Oxford, founded a priory at Hedingham and was three times married; his third wife Lucy produced two sons to follow their father as second and third Earls. Aubrey died in 1194 and was buried in Colne priory. Aubrey's second son Robert, 3rd Earl of Oxford, was one of the barons who was party to the introduction of the Magna Carta, present at Runnymede in June 1215 where King John agreed to read and seal the great charter, much to his secret displeasure. Later the document was annulled by the Pope; who also excommunicated the barons involved; they fled to their castles when King John went on the rampage. Colchester and Stansted were attacked, Hedingham came under siege in 1216 by John and his French mercenaries, falling into their hands after the soldiers in the castle surrendered, exhausted after the long siege. Later that year King John died and his young son Henry III came to the throne. Robert and the other barons involved in the confrontation with his father had their castles and titles returned to them. Robert married Isabella de Bolebec and had a son Hugh, who succeeded to the titles and estates of his father when Robert died in 1221. He was buried in the priory at Hatfield Broad Oak, which was founded by the first earl in 1135; his stone effigy can be seen in the present day church of St Mary the Virgin.

The line of the Earls of Oxford continued as crusaders, soldiers and diplomats and as the hereditary Chamberlains of England. They distinguished themselves in battles and as members of the king's court serving Edward I to Edward III. John, the 7th Earl, fought as a commander at the battle of Crécy in 1346 with the Black Prince, in what was later called the Hundred Years War (1337-1453). John was a soldier, a brave fighting man and one of the king's most reliable generals, fighting at sea as well as on land. He died in 1360 during a campaign in Burgundy; his body was brought home and buried in Colne priory. He left a widow, Maud, and four sons and a daughter. In his will he left money (1000 marks) as a dowry for his daughter's wedding and money for the upkeep of Colne church.

The 9th Earl Robert, was a child when he inherited the title Earl of Oxford. He was born in 1362 and only 9 when his father Thomas, the 8th Earl, died in 1371. Robert was knighted by Edward III in 1377 when he was only 15, and married Philippa, daughter of the Earl of Bedford the following year. Richard II was now king and close friendship developed between the King and Robert as they were about the same age. In 1381 the people of Essex and Kent were in revolt over poll taxes and had marched to London, led by Wat Tyler, to meet the king at Smithfield to talk terms of agreement, Robert was at the king's side throughout the confrontation. In a heated exchange with the Mayor of London Tyler was killed and the crowd dispersed, Robert and the other nobles with the king returned to the Tower. The Peasants' Revolt was soon over and the people paid a high price for their act of defiance; many were hunted down and hung from the nearest tree or killed in skirmishes with the king's men. The king was under the influence of his uncles, but wanted to be independent of them and rule the country with the help of friends like Michael de la Pole, the Earl of Suffolk, and Robert de Vere, the Earl of Oxford. The king was generous to Robert with awards and honours, conferring on him the title Duke of Ireland. He accumulated much wealth that went with the office; he was also given custody of Colchester town and Castle, was made a member of the Privy Council and Knight of the Garter, much to the envy of the other nobles. Robert was making enemies. Rumours were circulating in court about Robert's relationship with the king, and many were hoping he would be sent to Ireland

Robert was to stay as the king's favourite and was given the royal castle at Berkhamstead as a residence. Robert's mistake was to offend the Duke of Gloucester by abandoning his wife Philippa (the Duke's niece) for one of the Queen's servants. Problems were gathering around the king as Gloucester and his friends the Lords Appellants were aiming to rid the king of his friends and advisors. Robert was accused of treason by the Appellants and all his estates and properties were taken from him. He was able to make an escape to Chester where he raised a small army of men and marched towards London. An army led by the Earl of Arundel met Robert at Radcot in Oxfordshire, on a bridge over the Thames. But Robert's army fled before Arundel's advance, abandoning Robert and shouting "traitor, traitor". Robert escaped across the river and made his way to London to try and see the king. After a brief stay in London, Robert said farewell to Richard and sailed for the continent, heading for Bruges where he had some money in the city's bank.

Meanwhile in London, the Merciless Parliament was called by the Lords Appellant accusing Robert de Vere, Earl of Oxford, and others of treason. Accusing him in his absence of having control over the king, offering bad advice on foreign affairs, excessive and unnecessary spending from the exchequer, failing to understand common and statute law. These and many other personal charges were levelled at Robert, covering the time he was in office and had the ear of the king. He was found guilty along with several others including Alexander Neville, the Archbishop of York, and Michael de la Pole, who had fled to Paris. They were all sentenced to death by the Merciless Parliament, so-called because of the harsh sentences it inflicted in 1388. Robert lived in exile along with the other fugitives in extreme poverty and distress. He did not live to see King Richard avenge his friends, when in 1397 the Lords Appellant were abolished, and the members arrested and banished. Some were executed including the king's uncle, the Duke of Gloucester.

Robert had died in 1392; he been out hunting wild boar when the beast they were stalking turned and attacked him, inflicting wounds from which he later died. King Richard, several years later had Robert's remains brought back to England and buried at Colne The king attended the funeral along with Robert's mother and a few friends; Richard was deeply moved by the death of his friend. Robert left a wife but no children, so the title Earl of Oxford went to his uncle, Aubrey de Vere, who became the 10th Earl. While his nephew was a royal favourite, Aubrey had been given custody of Hadleigh Castle, a manor in Thundersley, and revenue from the town and Castle of Rayleigh. He received all the titles and properties lost through the Merciless Parliament, including the title Earl of Oxford, but not the hereditary title and office, Great Chamberlain of England. This was lost with the death of Robert for several generations until the 13th Earl had the title restored to the family by Henry VII in 1485.

John, the 13th Earl of Oxford, was born in 1443 to John, the 12th Earl, and Elizabeth Howard. His father and brother were executed on Tower Hill in 1462 for supporting the Lancastrian cause, Edward IV (a Yorkist) was king, Henry VI was now interned in the Tower of London. These were troubled times, for this was the time of civil war in England, later known as the Wars of the Roses, a name that hides the horror of a war that stalked the countryside for over thirty years. One of Edward's first acts as king was to deal severely with any Lancastrian resistance - that was when John's father and brother were arrested and executed.

John was treated with suspicion by King Edward due to the family connections with the Lancastrian cause, and eventually found himself in the Tower of London as a prisoner in 1468 on the king's orders. After his release he joined Richard Neville, Earl of Warwick 'the king maker', who for many years had fought and championed the Yorkist cause.   However, he was now disillusioned with King Edward's rule and incensed when the king secretly married Elizabeth Woodville, a Lancastrian widow. Warwick was campaigning to replace Edward with the old King Henry who for many years had been under arrest and held in the Tower. John de Vere, Earl of Oxford, Richard Neville, Earl of Warwick, and the Duke of Clarence, the king's brother, rose against Edward, killing a number of the queen's relatives and holding the king hostage at Middleham Castle, a Neville stronghold in the North. When he was released by Warwick, Edward turned on his captors sending them fleeing to the continent. Warwick joined his old enemy, Margaret of Anjou, returned to England. and reinstated Henry VI to the throne. Edward rallied his supporters and marched to meet them. Meanwhile, Clarence and the king had become reconciled and moved together against Warwick. John, the Earl of Oxford, had gathered an army and was marching to join the Lancastrians.

The armies met at Barnet on the 14th April 1471. The morning broke very foggy, so the two armies only had limited visibility. The king's forces had Edward and Clarence centre, with Richard, Duke of Gloucester, to his right and Lord Hastings to his left. On the opposing side, Warwick was to the rear of Sir John Neville, the Marquis of Montagu (Warwick's brother), the Earl of Oxford to Montagu's right and the Earl of Exeter to the left. The scene was set for bloody conflict. The fog prevented the sides meeting in a head on clash; as both armies moved forward Montagu and Edward met first and attacked with sword and pike. Oxford charged forward to attack Lord Hastings' flank and quickly routed Hastings' men, breaking up the ranks of soldiers who turned and fled the battlefield. The Earl of Oxford could not stop his men charging on to the village of Barnet and looting it. The battle raged on in the fog, and because of movement of troops and hand to hand fighting, the battle line turned. Meanwhile Oxford had gathered his men together and was making his way back to the battlefield. He charged into what he thought were Edward's men, but a terrible mistake was made in the fog. Oxford's cavalry rode into Sir John Neville's men who mistook the de Vere star (a badge or emblem worn on their tunics) for Edward's badge, a sun.   In the confusion Montague archers started firing on Oxford's men who shouted, "Treason, treason", thinking treachery had taken place. Panic overtook Oxford's men and they fled the battlefield. The Lancastrian line started to collapse, Warwick in heavy armour was fighting on foot having been separated from his horse. He was surrounded by Edward's men and killed. The Marquis of

Montagu, Sir John Neville, was also killed; York had won the day. The Earl of Oxford spurred his horse and fled from the battle heading for Scotland and safety.

A victorious Edward marched to London with the bodies of Warwick and his brother John, and put them on show at St Paul's Cathedral. John de Vere, the 13th Earl of Oxford, was now an outlaw. He had reached France after the battle of Barnet and had recruited a small band of followers who attacked the English coast and harassed Yorkist ships. He was pursued to Cornwall where he and his band of renegades took refuge in St Michael's Mount. There he was held to siege by Edward's men for several months, eventually surrendering and was then confined to a French prison.

Three years went by for John de Vere languishing in a French jail until he managed to escape in 1484. King Edward IV had died suddenly in 1483 and Richard, Duke of Gloucester, was made protector of King Edward's sons, Edward aged 12 and his brother, Richard of York. They later disappeared from the Tower of London, and the Duke of Gloucester was crowned Richard III; the Yorkists were still in power. Richard was unpopular in the south of England and suspicion fell on him regarding the young princes' fate in the Tower. Also several murders of men of rank were committed and Richard's name was linked to these events. A popular rhyme of the day, sung in the streets went:

> The cat, the rat and Lovell our dog
> Rule all England under a hog.

This was in reference to Richard's ministers, William Catesby, Richard Ratcliffe and Lord Lovel. Richard was 'the hog' due to his badge or emblem, which was a boar. John de Vere, still a staunch Lancastrian, would not accept Richard as king and made his way to Milford Haven in south-west Wales where Henry Tudor, Earl of Richmond, had arrived with several thousand fighting men to challenge King Richard. Henry Tudor welcomed the Earl of Oxford's support and made him commander of his army, marching inland to meet King Richard at Bosworth in Leicestershire on the 22nd August 1485

John de Vere's skill on the battlefield greatly assisted Henry Tudor in obtaining a victory at Bosworth. King Richard III was killed and Henry Tudor crowned on the battlefield as the new King of England, Henry VII. He showed his gratitude to John de Vere by giving back all the titles and honours that he had lost under the Yorkist rule, including the hereditary Chamberlainship of England, which had been lost to the family by Robert, the 9th Earl in 1392.

John prospered under Henry VII and became a wealthy man from the revenue and titles he received. The family home, Hedingham Castle, was in a poor state of repair. John's wife had been reduced almost to poverty while John was outlawed but now wealth and status were back with the De Veres. An extensive building programe now took place at Hedingham. Several buildings were constructed in the inner bailey and a red brick bridge built over the moat, which the visitor walks over today when visiting the keep. An incident in 1498, when King Henry VII visited John and his wife at the castle at Hedingham, was to cause financial problems for the de Veres for many years. John, who was anxious to please and impress the king, had all the castle retinue line the route to the castle wearing their finest livery. He then entertained the king for a week, providing the very best in food and wine. At the end of the king's stay at Hedingham, Henry, who by now had a reputation as a miser, was not impressed by the show of wealth and fined de Vere 15,000 marks for breaking a law that stated that nobles could only have a certain number of retainers. The Earl of Oxford's comments were not recorded!

John continued with his duties at Hedingham and as high steward for the king until he died on the 10th March 1513 aged 70, a good age for this man of action. He was buried at Earls Colne Priory with his first wife. His only son had died in the Tower of London while John was exiled in France. The titles passed to John, his brother's son, who then became the 14th Earl.

John was 12 when his uncle died. He was made the ward of King Henry VIII and lived under the guardianship of Cardinal Thomas Wolsey. In 1520 John inherited his uncle's titles and estates and accepted the title 14th Earl of Oxford. John married Ann Howard and lived such an expensive and extravagant lifestyle that his money was soon squandered. He was ordered to relinquish the management of his estates to Cardinal Wolsey. John died in 1526 aged 27; there were no children from his loveless marriage.

The 15th Earl (1490-1540), also named John, was cousin to the 14th Earl. He was knighted by Henry VIII after the Battle of the Spurs on 16th August, 1513. John fought alongside King Henry and the Emperor Maximilian against the French at Guinegate. King Henry had a strong force of 30,000 men and routed the French cavalry, who fled the battlefield losing their spurs in the flight. John was made a Knight of the Garter in 1527. King Henry was married to Catherine of Aragon, his brother's widow; they had been married for over 24 years and had lost 5 children stillborn or dead within a few days of birth. One daughter survived, Mary. Henry was becoming increasingly frustrated that he had no son from his marriage with Catherine, and using the excuse that God had not blessed his marriage his eyes started wandering over the ladies of the court. Mary Boleyn, the king's mistress, had a sister Anne whom the king met, and being smitten by her beauty, wanted to marry. Cardinal Wolsey was given the task of arranging Henry's divorce from Catherine with the Pope in Rome. When he failed he was charged with treason. John, the 15th Earl of Oxford, was appointed investigating officer against the Cardinal, who died before he came to trial. The Pope was unwilling to gratify King Henry's request for divorce, so Henry broke from Rome and became 'Supreme Head of the Church of England' annulling his own marriage with Catherine of Aragon in 1533, so allowing him to marry Ann

Boleyn. John, Earl of Oxford, carried the crown at her coronation and later attended at her trial when she was charged with adultery and executed in 1536. John was in attendance at court for two of Henry's other wives, Jane Seymour, who died in childbirth, and Ann of Cleves, the least favoured wife of the king. John was in the king's party when they went to receive Ann at Rochester in Kent. The king was not best pleased with 'this Flanders Mare'. This meeting was arranged for King Henry by Thomas Cromwell, who advised that it would be a good political marriage, but Ann was lacking the beauty and grace of Ann Boleyn and Jane Seymour. The wedding took place in January 1540 and was annulled that same year.

John, the 15th Earl, married Elizabeth Trussel and had four sons and four daughters. John died in 1540; his black marble tomb can be seen in St Nicholas Church in Castle Hedingham village.

The 16th Earl of Oxford, also named John (1512-62), was the eldest son and inherited all the titles and offices of his predecessors, including hereditary title of Great Chamberlain. He was knighted by King Edward VI in 1547. When the young King Edward died, John supported the Princess Mary against Lady Jane Gray in a power struggle for the throne. Mary became queen and John attended the Coronation as sword bearer. Mary's reign ended in 1558 after 5 years of an unsuccessful attempt to restore the old faith (Roman Catholicism) in the country. This had led to the persecution and burning of Protestants, which gave her the nickname 'Bloody Mary'. Her sister Elizabeth succeeded to the throne and John attended the Queen at her Coronation. He was given many appointments by Elizabeth and attended the Queen's court to officiate in state affairs. The 16th Earl was a keen sportsman and excelled in hawking and hunting. Elizabeth visited the Earl of Oxford at Castle Hedingham and stayed for five days in August 1561. The visit must have cost John a small fortune as the Queen travelled with a large retinue and many a household had been financially ruined after one of Elizabeth's visits. John died in 1562 having married twice. His first wife was Lady Dorothy Neville, the daughter of Ralph, the 4th Earl of Westmorland; his second wife was Margaret Golding, who gave birth to Edward and Mary, John's son and daughter.

Edward became the 17th Earl (1550-1604). Edward was 12 when his father died and William Cecil, (later Lord Burghley) was made his guardian, while his uncle Arthur Golding was his tutor and also managed young Edward's estates and inherited titles. Edward was educated in William Cecil's house in London and was tutored in languages, music and dance, and excelled in sports for which he had a natural talent. But Edward had a quick temper and it often got him into trouble. In 1557 an incident took place in William Cecil's house that resulted in him being charged in court with stabbing the cook, who later died of his wounds. The jury found in Edward's favour with the extraordinary verdict of *felo de se* (self murder) saying in effect that the cook fell on the knife and subsequently died. Edward was released back to Sir William Cecil, but the quarrelling continued in the Cecil household, much to the frustration of all who fell foul of Edward's quick tongue. He went on to Oxford and Cambridge Universities to study law, and finally took his seat in the House of Lords in 1571.

Edward was an excellent horseman and was skilled in jousting at tournaments. It was at one of these meetings that he came to the attention of Queen Elizabeth, who was impressed with the young man, and he received from the Queen a prize for his prowess. He was soon attending Elizabeth's court and by all accounts was witty, fashionable, cultured in music and the arts, and handsome. He became a favourite with the Queen and was soon writing poems and verses for her, but life at court for Edward was becoming a chore. He was bored and restless and at this time married Lord Burghley's daughter Ann, but this union was far from a happy one, probably due to Edward's quarrelsome nature. He was fed up at court and wanted military service, but this was not granted so he ran away to Flanders without the Queen's permission. Elizabeth sent envoys to bring him back and Edward was reconciled with the Queen, at least on this occasion. Edward still longed for travel this time he was given permission to go to Italy and France returning after many months with gifts for the Queen; gloves, dresses, and perfumes, which greatly pleased her. Edward's marriage was under a lot of strain so he spent a great deal of time at court. His output of poems and plays was prolific at this time; several volumes of his poems were published and he produced and performed in his own plays. But his temper was to get the better of him again. In 1579 while playing tennis, he insulted Sir Philip Sidney and both agreed to a duel. The Queen intervened trying to make Sidney apologise; he refused, and left Elizabeth's court. Again in 1581 Edward fought a duel with Thomas Knyvet, a member of the Queen's Privy Council. Both men were wounded, but the feud continued via each other's friends and two men were killed in the actions that followed. The Queen was informed of the action by Edward's friends and he was placed under house arrest. The Queen pardoned him in 1583. In 1586 Edward was at last employed on official business as a special commissioner for the trial of Mary, Queen of Scots, at Fotheringay Castle, Northamptonshire. Mary was later executed at the Castle in 1587.

In 1588 the Spanish were preparing to invade England and a fleet of ships was put to sea to intercept them. Edward volunteered to sail with the English fleet and distinguished himself in battle. The Spanish fleet was routed and the English victorious. Edward had incurred many debts over the years and he started to sell off parts of the Earls Colne estates to his steward Roger Harlackenden. Lord Burghley had looked after Edward's wife and children while Edward was living his extravagant life style, mixing with artists and actors. Edward's wife died in 1588 and was buried in Westminster Abbey. Lord

Burghley was not inclined to help Edward out of his financial difficulties. Edward had squandered most of his own fortune and was living on charity from his friends. Edward was patron of an acting company and players known as 'the Earl of Oxford's boys'. They were always in debt and when Edward took lodgings in London often left without paying the bill. Edward was writing many poems and plays of quality, and there has been speculation and heated debate since 1920 that he might have been Shakespeare, due to Edward's early poems resembling Shakespeare's early works. Edward married again, this time to Elizabeth Trentham, one of the Queen's maids; they had one son, Henry. In 1592 Edward started an import business of fruits, oil and wool, but this failed. Elizabeth died in 1603 to be followed by the son of Mary, Queen of Scots, James I. Edward, as Earl of Oxford, officiated at the Coronation, then left the court and lived in Hackney, East London. He died 24 June 1604 and was buried in St Augustine's, Hackney. Edward's son, Henry, became the 18th Earl; he was a rebellious and troublesome youth.

He was educated at Oxford and was knighted into the Order of the Bath. He became the keeper of Havering Park, along with the office of Great Chamberlain. He inherited part of his mother's fortune and went on a foreign tour for five years, returning to England in 1618. He quarrelled with the Duke of Buckingham, which led to his imprisonment in the Tower of London. He was later released and married Lady Diana Cecil, who brought him her fortune. He went to the Hague and died of fever in 1625. His body was bought home and buried in Westminster Abbey.

There were no children and Castle Hedingham went to the Trentham family: his mother's side. The de Veres time as great estate and castle owners had now come to an end. Henry was succeeded by his second cousin Robert.

Robert, the 19th Earl of Oxford, lost the office of Great Chamberlain, after a three day debate in the House of Lords, to a rival claim from Lord Willoughby de Eresby. Robert went abroad with his cousin Sir Edward Vere and was a captain in the English army in Holland, and when Sir Edward was killed in battle in 1629 Robert was made colonel of his regiment. He too was fatally wounded and later died at the siege of Maastricht in 1632.

His son Aubrey became the 20th and the last Earl of Oxford. Aubrey's contribution was to establish the Horse Guards, that we see today on duty in Whitehall, and at other ceremonial occasions. In 1661 he was made colonel of a cavalry regiment with the nickname the Oxford Blues, called after him as he was the Earl of Oxford. When he died in 1703 they were called The Blues or The

Royals - now known as The Royal Horse Guards (the Blues). The title Earl of Oxford ended with Aubrey, when 20 generations of soldiers, statesmen, diplomats, and friends of kings came to an end.

The ancestral home at Castle Hedingham was sold in 1713 to Sir William Ashurst, Lord Mayor of London, who built a new red brick house near the Tudor bridge in part of the outer bailey. Most of the old buildings that surrounded the castle keep were falling down and in a dilapidated state. Sir William cleared the site and started to create gardens and a lake. His son Robert continued the work when father died in 1719, planting trees and enlarging the garden. Sir William's daughter Elizabeth inherited the house and castle when her brothers died. Later the Majendie family came into possession of the estate and lived and worked the estate until 1870 when, by various marriages a descendant of the de Vere family, Thomas Lindsay, came into possession of the castle. His father was descended from the 7th Earl John, and his mother had family connections from the 20th and last Earl of Oxford, so after many years the de Veres were once again by name back at Hedingham.

Today the castle is a tourist attraction, the great keep towering above the trees, grey and dominating the village at its feet, and can be seen for miles around. It is an ideal place for film makers looking for the right image for mediæval films. The TV serial *Ivanhoe* was shot here and re-enactors can often be seen at weekends creating mediæval life for the public, showing what life may have been like in past times. The castle is open in the summer and it is very pleasant to walk around the gardens and outer bailey woods, and to walk up the steps of the great keep, now well worn from the thousands of feet that over the centuries have entered the Norman doorway. Now not to be challenged by a sentry, but to savour the gentler side of modern life in the tea room!

For details of opening times and events 'phone: (01787) 460261

Recommended further reading. *The De Veres of Castle Hedingham* by Verily Anderson.

RAYLEIGH CASTLE
OS 178　　　　　　TQ 8091

The town of Rayleigh is 6 miles north west of Southend-on-Sea off the A127. The name Rayleigh is from the Saxon *(raa)* a buck or wild goat, and *(ley)* a pasture - not many wild goats around today, but a very pleasant and busy town. The castle is tucked away behind a windmill and a community hall at the end of Rayleigh High Street. It is now hard to recognise what it once was a Norman motte and bailey stronghold Today it is called Rayleigh Mount and looks like a small park and if you visit in the spring it is alive with daffodils. There is a tree ringed pond with resident ducks, walkers stroll with their dogs and children play on the grassy slopes. A path will take you round the course of the bailey, and wooden steps built into a steep hill will take you to the top of a 50 foot mound. You then stand where in Norman times the castle keep stood looking out over the Essex countryside. Inside the bailey lived the soldiers and the workforce that supported them - blacksmiths, bakers, butchers and livestock, all living as one large community under its Norman lord.

　　　　The castle was owned by Robert Fitz-Wymarc, landowner and friend of King Edward the Confessor. He was a steward at the royal court and one of the few Normans in high office that the Saxons trusted. Robert owned and lived at Clavering Castle in Essex, and when in the year 1052 the Saxon Earl Godwin and his family returned to England from exile after their quarrel with the King, the unpopular Normans in Edward's court fled to Robert's castle at Clavering and then back to Normandy. Robert remained at the king's court as Edward's friend and was no threat to Harold Godwin and his family.

Then in January 1066 the old King was dying, and in attendance at Westminster were Robert Fitz Wymarc, Earl Harold Godwin, Edith, Harold's sister and wife to King Edward, also Stigand, the Archbishop of Canterbury. They are depicted on the Bayeux Tapestry standing around the old king's bed. Robert is seen supporting Edward, helping him to sit up and talk to Harold. The king died on the 5th January 1066 and Harold was offered the crown of England. He was crowned king the following day, the 6th January, in Westminster Abbey.

When Robert died, his son Swein inherited the lands and estates in Essex including Rayleigh. Swein or Suene kept the favour of William as his father had done, and inherited his father's titles, and was given the name de Essex. He now made his home at Rayleigh and moved from his father's old home at Clavering.

He rebuilt and strengthened the castle and enlarged the area around it with vineyards and a hunting park. This was popular with the nobility for many years. Swein's son Robert inherited the castle and estates, and his son, Henry de Essex, inherited at the time of the civil war between Stephen and Matilda. Henry was an ally of Matilda, and when Henry II, Matilda's son, came to the throne in 1154, Henry de Essex became the king's standard bearer and Constable of England. However in 1157, during a battle with the Welsh, in the confusion the cry went up that the king was killed; Henry threw down the royal standard and fled the battlefield. Unfortunately for him the king was saved, so Henry de Essex was disgraced and had to defend his honour in trial by combat. Henry was badly injured, believed to be dying and was cared for by monks. He recovered, and remained with the monks in their abbey at Reading, where he died years later. His lands and castles were confiscated by the king and became crown property.

Many owners came and went, then in 1215 King John granted the estate of Rayleigh to Hubert de Burgh, Chief Justiciar of England and supporter of the king against the rebel barons when civil war broke out over Magna Carta. When John died in 1216, his son, then only nine years old, became King Henry III.

Hubert de Burgh became the king's adviser on foreign affairs and one of the most powerful men in England. Around the year 1230 Hubert was granted permission to build a castle at Hadleigh, and Rayleigh was gradually abandoned and fell into decay. About 1280 the Rayleigh lands passed to Eleanor, wife of Edward I. She used the land for a horse stud farm and breeding centre until she died in 1290.

Time passed and in 1394 Richard II gave permission for the stones from the castle to be removed by the local people; who used them to build the church tower. For many years the lands around the castle were used for grazing cattle, and by Tudor times the castle was called '*the ruin*'. The Normans, the Angevins and the Plantagenets lived here and left their mark. All has now gone, except a few visible remains and a memory of what was once home to powerful men and friends of kings

Today the motte and bailey covers about two acres and is in the care of the National Trust; a guide book describing the complex structure of the old castle is available from the adjoining hall. Around the earthworks information boards are placed at points of interest, with details of the history and management of the mount; access is free and a car park is nearby.

HADLEIGH CASTLE
OS 178   TQ 8186

Hadleigh, the Saxon word *head* high and *ley* pasture (high pasture)) is in Thames-side Essex near Southend-on-Sea, off the A13 London to Southend road. If you drive down Castle Lane to reach the castle, beware. The road gets very narrow at the end of the lane as you come to a dead end; leave the car and go over a stile then it is a short walk to the castle.

A visit to the ruins of Hadleigh Castle any summer weekend is far from peaceful, you will not be alone! This windswept part of Essex, overlooking the Thames estuary and marsh land, attracts in large numbers, the hikers, cyclists, picnickers, kite flyers and dog walkers. Kids climb over the walls and ignore the *'keep off the wall'* signs. The attraction is understandable as you stand by the old round tower and look over the landscape.

To your left is Old Leigh and Westcliff-on-Sea, the river Thames winds its way east from London glinting in the distance, the sun shines off the mud flats and a train on the Southend to Fenchurch line, looking like a toy, rumbles past in the downland way below you. In the distance on the river the occasional sail of a Thames sailing barge passes by; sometimes the scene changes and tankers and bulk carriers, barely moving as you watch, make their way to Tilbury.

This is a nice place to be on a sunny day; there are views, windy old ruins, grass to sit on and have a picnic, but the time to come here is in the winter when there is not a soul about. Walk up the grassy slopes of the old earthworks and stand by the gray drum tower among the fallen walls of the once great castle. On a dark brooding day, clouds heavy and threatening, waiting to drop torrents of rain - you feel the spirit and the menace of the castle guarding the Thames estuary and the approaches to London. This was one of the last Norman castles to be built, about the year 1230. Its aim was to stop French invaders and raiders from approaching London and attacking shipping in the Thames. The castle was built by the colourful character who served King John and King Henry III, Hubert de Burgh, Chief Justice of England and a great land owner.

Hubert came from humble origins in Norfolk, but went on to become the most powerful man in England under King Henry III, until his downfall in 1232. Hubert came to prominence in the court of King John, who was quick to recognise ambition and talent in military and administrative matters. Hubert soon rose to power with the king as his friend. In 1215 Hubert played a part in drawing up the terms of Magna Carta, but remained loyal to King John when in 1216 the barons were in revolt over the king's disregard of the terms of the great charter. Some barons planned to replace the king with Prince Louis of France, son of Philip II. War broke out and Hubert was sent to Dover Castle to protect the south coast from French mercenaries.

The castle was under siege for many months, but Hubert held it against the French with just a few men, while King John was campaigning around the country against the rebel Barons and the French. The toll was to tell on the king, who, after many months of war and a short illness, died in 1217, while Hubert was still defending Dover. Messages were sent to the Dover defenders about the king's death and the succession of his son, so Hubert made terms with Prince Louis for a temporary truce and went to London.

The new king, who became Henry III, was only nine when his father died, so the ageing William Marshal was given the job of regent to govern during the infancy of the boy king. Meanwhile the French were at sea waiting to invade with a large fleet of ships and many soldiers. Hubert was preparing to meet the French with ships gathered from the south coast and men from Dover and the Cinque Ports. A great naval battle was fought and the French invaders routed. Hubert returned a hero, and peace settled over England.

In 1219 William Marshal died and Hubert de Burg became regent in his place. He quickly established his influence over the young king, giving him sound advice and helping young Henry through the early days of his reign. The rewards from this position were many. He became Earl of Kent, Sheriff of seven counties, constable of three Welsh castles, and had estates in fifteen counties.

Over a period of time he married three rich widows, and finally married Princess Margaret, the sister of the King of Scotland. Hubert took up residence in the White Tower within the Tower of London and lived comfortably, but all was not well within the court circle. Hubert was making enemies and causing resentment amongst the other barons because of his power and wealth.

By 1227 Henry was twenty and decided to rule without Hubert's help. This left Hubert vulnerable to attack from the other barons who saw him losing power, so stories and rumours were fed to Henry about Hubert's wealth. It was also said that he had given bad advice to the young king when he was regent. Hubert denied these rumours and continued to support Henry in affairs of state.

In 1228 Henry III wanted funds for an expedition to regain lost lands in France, but Hubert was against the plan. It would be an unpopular venture and expensive, but the king insisted and Hubert had the unenviable task of raising the money. The venture was a disaster. Men and ships were in short supply, so the king accused Hubert of incompetence and called him a traitor. It was the start of Hubert's downfall. The building of Hadleigh Castle was started about this time with permission from the king, and Hubert was responsible for its construction. Kentish ragstone was shipped in, with workmen and masons and all the support services needed to construct a mediæval castle, no easy task as it was on a steep hill on windswept marshes.

The castle was to be for the defence of London and a baronial home. Unlike other early Norman castles, no central keep was included in the plan of the castle.

Thick high walls and round towers, state rooms and kitchens were built around a large courtyard, with an entrance through a barbican, and around the castle were earth banks and ditches. There is no evidence to suggest that Hubert de Burgh was about to move into the castle. He was probably just the overseer for its construction. But he had problems, as charges of corruption were made against him by barons jealous of his power and wealth, and the king was ready to believe anything bad about Hubert, as he still blamed him for the failure of the French campaign. Hubert was living in London and decided to move out into the country until things quietened down.

On his way to Norfolk where his wife was staying, Hubert stopped at Brentwood, but in the night, agents of his accusers recognised him and tried to arrest him. Hubert then fled into Becket's chapel, a church for pilgrims on their way to Canterbury. He claimed sanctuary but was dragged out and was about to be bound with iron shackles, when the blacksmith summoned to fetter him recognised Hubert and refused to bind him. Hubert was then taken back to London bound to his horse.

The Bishop of London was outraged that sanctuary had been broken, and allowed Hubert to return to the chapel at Brentwood where he stayed for many months. When he left the chapel he was interned in the Tower of London where he stayed for several years. King Henry III was unforgiving and confiscated all his lands and castles, leaving Hubert to contemplate his future.

Hubert was reinstated to the court several years later, but with failing health and more accusations brought against him. He died worn out and disillusioned in 1243. Hubert was a man of his time, ruthless, ambitious, and powerful, but, like all such men in history, they have had their day and leave us their story. After Hubert's death Hadleigh castle was kept by the king as a grace and favour residence, but little was done to maintain it. Some repairs had to be made in 1256, but the castle gradually fell into disuse.

The years passed and in the reign of Edward III conflict with France resumed. With the threat of French raids in the Thames estuary, Edward commissioned extensive refurbishment of the castle around the year 1365. Two great drum towers were built, a new gateway and barbican to a large courtyard, state rooms and kitchens, all built to make the castle more comfortable. The walls were strengthened, earth banks and ditches were raised and cleared of rubble. Soon the castle stood four square and solid, a formidable barrier to London for any potential invader. However, Hadleigh never saw any enemies at the gates, sieges or battles, so it spent its remaining years as a comfortable residence for its many owners.

Its disintegration began in 1552 when King Edward VI sold the castle and land. The new owner started to demolish the castle for its Reigate stone, and sold it as building materials; by the end of the 16th century the castle was a ruin. Over the years wind and rain, landslips and time have taken their toll. Today the remains of the great drum towers and walls, built by Edward III and immortalised by the artist John Constable, are all that remain of the mighty castle, and the men and women who once lived and died here are just memories in the history books.

COLCHESTER CASTLE
OS 168   TL 0025

Colchester is built on a hill overlooking the Colne river. This was an ancient place even before the Romans came, a town with over 2000 years of history, proudly displaying a large sign on approach roads saying, 'Colchester - the oldest recorded town'. A garrison town with modern shops, museums, a splendid town hall, and visible Roman remains, but at the very heart of the town is the castle. It was built by the Normans and was one of the first two castles to be built of stone, the other being the Tower of London.

The Colchester story starts long before the Normans came in 1066. The Normans were the last to conquer and occupy England, but the Romans were the first to come to these shores and subjugate the people and their lands. In 55BC Julius Caesar was the first to arrive with an army, exploratory raids at first, later full occupation when the Emperor Claudius arrived in 43AD.

A Celtic tribe the Trinovantes, lived in the area we now call Essex, their capital was Camulodunum, named after Camulos, the Celtic war god. Not a town yet but an extended settlement over a wide area, with protective earth banks and ditches. The Romans built a town with shops and houses using stone and brick as their building material. A thousand years before the castle was built a great Roman temple dedicated to the Emperor Claudius stood on the site.

It was here in AD60 that the warrior Queen Boudicca swept into the Roman town at the head of a large army of Celtic warriors to destroy the temple and kill any Roman citizen or soldier that stood in their way. The temple was destroyed, many people killed, and the town reduced to a burning pile of rubble. The Celtic army moved on to Londinium (London), then Verulamium (St Albans), burning and killing as they made their way around the countryside. Eventually the Romans gained control of the situation, Boudicca dying by her own hand after watching her army defeated in battle. After the Celtic revolt Colchester was rebuilt along with the other towns that were destroyed in the madness of the revolution.

The temple too was rebuilt and soon the town was flourishing again with shops and houses, but around the town the Romans built a strong wall with gates to protect the citizens from any further attacks. The Roman occupation lasted 400 years and the visitor can see the remains of that great era around the town today. A new invasion was now threatening England, the Picts and the Scots from beyond the great Roman wall on the Scottish borders started to move south. Other raiders arrived from the sea, not from the Mediterranean this time, but men from the North. Germanic peoples - the Saxons, Angles and Jutes - and seamen warriors from Scandinavia, the Vikings, all came to Britain to plunder and kill the unprotected population. They arrived in the fifth and following centuries and settled around the country, the Angles in the north and east, the Jutes in the west and south of England.

The Vikings, warlike and terrifying, swept through the country attacking the monasteries, stealing their gold and silver and killing the monks, and making life miserable for the people in the villages. But life went on in this *'dark age'* period – 'dark' due to very little written history at this time. Minor wars broke out over land and the difficult integration of the emerging cultures that were now making the new Britain. Great leaders, men of their time, emerged over the ninth and tenth centuries to hold a divided England together from the troublesome Danes. Leaders like Alfred the Great (802-900) and Edgar the Peaceful (959-75) were able to unite the country and bring the Danes under control. The eleventh century saw the Danish King Canute become king of England (1016-35); he became a Christian and the land settled into a peaceful state. The fighting had stopped and the Danes, who for so long had caused many problems, had now settled down to farm and raise families.

By 1066 Anglo-Saxon England was established as a settled, cultured land. Harold II was the King, the country was at peace, but threats of war were coming from Normandy; invasion was imminent. Then on the 14th October 1066 England had a new master, William, Duke of Normandy. The Saxon Harold was dead. The Normans had arrived soon establishing themselves in the counties of England taking the Saxon lands for themselves.

Saxon Colchester was a prosperous place with a port and a population living within the Roman walls, which were still standing. They had been repaired in 917 but most of the old Roman town was by now a ruin. The Saxons were not great builders, so many of the roads and houses were in a dilapidated state. They did not use the buildings they had inherited from the past, but a Saxon tower and doorway still survive today at Holy Trinity Church.

The Normans arrived in earnest and settled themselves in the town. William, the new King of England, ordered that a castle be built near the important harbour at Hythe to protect the southern approaches to East Anglia. Work began about 1076 after Danish raids in 1072. The task of supervising the work was given to Eudo Dapifer, William's steward. As the town stood on the remains of a Roman city there were plenty of building materials freely available and other supplies were brought in from France.

The architect was probably Gundulf, a monk from Normandy, later Bishop of Rochester. He was skilled in working with stone and was building the White Tower (the Tower of London) at the same time as Colchester; later he built Rochester Castle and Cathedral and was in great demand for his skills. Colchester Castle was built over the foundations of the Roman temple, which had been left as a ruin. Years of wind and rain, and the locals taking stone for building, had left a large flat area with solid foundations, later exploited by the Normans. The temple vaults can still be seen on a guided tour of the castle.

Colchester was from the start a royal castle in the possession of the king; it was granted with its lands and income from time to time to various governors or military commanders, appointed by the king. Colchester Castle when completed had one of the largest stone keeps ever built by the Normans, 152 feet long, 110 feet wide, standing three storeys high with square towers at each corner to about 100 feet high with battlements and small arched windows. The original entrance was in the north wall, reached by a wooden stairway. This door was later blocked and a new large, arched entrance in the south wall was built with zig-zag patterns, a portcullis, and a great wooden door. This is the entrance visitors use today. Inside a wide stone spiral staircase led to the living apartments and great hall with great arched fireplaces decorated with herring bone pattern, all the comforts of home! Also here was all the other domestic accommodation for the castle household. There are some interesting carvings and graffiti on the walls and staircase. Some date from the 14th century, scratched on the wall by the bored soldiers, others made by members of the household that served in the great castle. Some were made by the many prisoners that were kept in the castle over the years. It is hard to imagine the fear the castle instilled in the local population. The prospect of ending up in one of its cells, as many did for debts and stealing, or as prisoners after battles was daunting. Some of the saddest groups were the men and women persecuted for their religious beliefs. They were held in dark cells until they were brought to trial, then burnt at the stake in the castle grounds.

Outside in Castle Park can be seen the defensive earthworks of the northern ramparts, and in the summer they are full of flowers, much admired by the thousands of visitors who visit the town and castle each year.

The castle was continually strengthened and enlarged over the years due to threats to William's new kingdom from abroad, and rebellions at home. Like all good Norman castles, Colchester was built to protect soldiers, administer the area and remind the citizens who was master now.

In 1089 William II made Eudo Dapifer, his steward, governor of the castle and town of Colchester. He was a just and popular administrator who founded the Abbey of St John and the leper hospital of Mary Magdalen. After a long life serving three Kings of England he died in 1120 and is buried in St John's Abbey.

The estates given to Eudo were only for his lifetime, so on his death the castle became the property of the crown, now Henry I (1100-35). The years 1135-54 saw the civil wars between Stephen and Matilda. The constable of the castle was Hamon St Clare who held the castle for Stephen, despite Queen Matilda's grant of the castle to Aubrey De Vere in 1141. The castle saw no action during the civil war and Hamon remained the constable until his death in 1150. He was succeeded by his son Hubert St Clare, who was custodian for only five years until his death in 1155.

Over the years various nobles held the castle in the king's name; it had started to deteriorate and money was needed to spend on repairs. Then in November 1214 King John (1199-1216) visited the castle. The custodian then was William de Lanvalai III whose family had been castellans since 1196. John distrusted de Lanvalai and had him replaced by one of his own men, Matthew Mantell. He was quickly replaced by Stephen Harengood, who restocked and made repairs to the castle installing several *ballistae,* huge mounted crossbows that could fire a missile up to 300 metres. Later Stephen Harengood left the castle and William de Lanvalai was reinstated, to John's cost at a later date.

In 1215, civil war was pending between King John and the barons over the terms and content of a great charter that had been presented to John and de Lanvalai was one of the rebellious barons. The list of demands that formed the great charter (Magna Carta) was drawn up by the barons, mainly to protect their own interests, but also to curb the abuse of royal power. King John was forced to meet the barons at Runnymead on 15th June 1215 and agree to its terms.

The documents were signed and sealed, and John and the barons departed. It is said of John that when he returned to Windsor Castle he went into such a rage that he fell to the floor foaming at the mouth, shouting curses and kicking the furniture, pure anger at the humiliation he had just endured from the barons. The king had no intention of honouring the terms agreed, and the charter was later annulled by the Pope. The barons declared war on the king and fled to their castles. In January 1216, French mercenaries were sent to England by the French Prince Louis to help the rebel barons, and a contingent went to Colchester and moved into the castle with William de Lanvalai. King John and his army marched to Suffolk, then Essex, and seized Framlingham Castle and Hedingham Castle after a short siege. Meanwhile John sent the French soldier Savory de Meulon, one of his trusted knights, to Colchester Castle to flush out the rebels. The castle and its defenders held out for three months under siege conditions, then submitted to the king in the month of March. The French soldiers were marched out and were allowed to depart, but the English were held to ransom and William de Lanvalai was removed from office.

The strain of the war and ill health brought about King John's death in Newark Castle on 18th October 1216; so ended a turbulent chapter in the castle's history and the loss of one of the more interesting kings, faults and all!

A succession of constables and sheriffs came and went as custodians of the castle, including Hubert de Burgh, who built Hadleigh castle, and Richard de Mountfitchet. Richard had lost his castle at Stansted in 1215 to King John in the civil war that followed Magna Carta. By 1350 Colchester castle was losing its status as an important defensive building, and was in a poor state of repair, and was used as the town jail.

The population was growing as the town prospered. There was a flourishing port through which wool was traded with the continent, also shoe making and tanning were major industries of the town. Later that same year the people suffered from the Black Death, a disease carried by rats. It was spread by fleas, biting man and infecting the bloodstream. It spread from the continent to London, then into the provinces. Colchester lost over a thousand souls to the disease, but a year later the town appeared to recover, and soon became prosperous again.

During the troubled reign of Henry VI, the Wars of the Roses (1455-85) raged throughout the country. The town and castle were unaffected by dynastic squabbles between York and Lancaster and the mismanagement of the country's affairs by the barons.

The castle was later given to Margaret of Anjou, the king's wife, who was responsible for perpetuating the war when her husband was incapacitated by bouts of madness. She wanted to secure her son's (Prince Edward) inheritance to the Lancastrian throne. Prince Edward was killed at the battle of Tewksbury by Yorkist troops and Queen Margaret captured. She then spent some time in the

Tower of London, where her husband King Henry IV was later murdered, the crown passing to Edward IV in 1461.

Edward was the second son of Cicely Neville and the Duke of York, Margaret's bitter enemy. Now the house of York held the throne of England.

Queen Margaret eventually went to France. where she died in 1482 and is buried in Angers Cathedral. From Margaret the castle went into the custody of Sir John Howard, later 1st Duke of Norfolk and follower of Richard III. Howard fought at the battle of Bosworth, August 1485, but was killed leading the advance guard with his son, who was captured by Henry Tudor and spent some time as a prisoner, but was later pardoned and his title restored as Duke of Norfolk. Fighting in the Tudor army with Henry was Sir John de Vere, who later became the custodian of Colchester Castle.

The de Vere family, the Earls of Oxford, had many estates in Essex and surrounding counties, building their castle home at Hedingham. It is worth noting that the many owners, great barons and lords who over the years had been the custodians of the castle and received its revenues, did not necessarily live there. A visit on the odd occasion to inspect the property, and at special occasions was in order; usually they had their family home elsewhere and the castle was just a source of revenue for them.

By 1600 the castle was in a poor state of repair and for many years had been used a prison, first being used as a jail in the 12th century. Buildings in the bailey had been used but as they were almost falling down through lack of maintenance prisoners kept escaping. Later prisoners were kept within the castle walls. Over the years many types of prisoners were held awaiting trial among them the vicar of Coggeshall, held for illegally fishing in the Abbey ponds! Other offences punished ranged from breaking forest laws to drunkenness.

Less fortunate were the Jews, who were held prisoners in 1253 by order of Henry III and suffered as a people for years under many kings. French knights were held for ransom after the battle of Crécy 1346, Scottish soldiers after the battle of Pinkie 1547 and Dutch prisoners in the reign of Charles II in 1653. The castle held Protestants under Queen Mary (1553-8) and Catholics under Elizabeth's rule (1558-1603); each group suffering death by burning at the stake for their beliefs. Men and women were held together in a cell in appalling conditions to reflect on their fate, then taken from the castle to die for their faith under the public gaze.

Another group of unfortunates were poor women held at Colchester during the reign of Charles I (1625-49) by the notorious witch hunter, Matthew Hopkins. His vocation was to interrogate and extract confessions from old or confused women and make them confess to practising witchcraft. Often the women's neighbours complained about something trivial, or women were perceived to be acting suspiciously. Then Hopkins was sent for and the women were put on trial. One such case at Colchester in 1645 was 15 year old Rebecca West, who was charged with witchcraft and held in prison with her mother Ann. During imprisonment Rebecca was bullied and threatened by Hopkins and his assistant to confess to the charges. She broke down probably through fear, and gave evidence against her mother and several other women saying they were witches. All were later hanged, and Hopkins moved on to find more victims in East Anglia. Hopkins was able to operate his interrogation skills with the knowledge that his actions were accepted, as society changed morally and spiritually due to the war with the king. This was part of the Puritan philosophy for a stricter moral code. The Puritans were extreme Protestants with a harsh attitude towards personal behaviour, and they abstained from any form of pleasure. They came to prominence during the Civil Wars. They were opposed to the monarchy, and any form of church ritual. They became identified with the Parliamentary cause which opposed the king's policies.

The Royalists, usually major land holders and true to the old faith, supported the king as absolute ruler. But in 1645 the royalists were losing the war, the king was in the custody of the Scots, and the assize courts had been suspended. The country was in a state of confusion and chaos, due to the many political and social changes, which had come about as a result of the war. In the south east the people affiliated themselves with the Parliamentarians and Matthew Hopkins the self-proclaimed Witchfinder General was called upon to root out so called 'evil practices' in the new moral climate. To say that witchcraft was to blame for the moral decline or attacks on the church, was just an excuse to blame the weak and vulnerable in society rather than themselves with their self-righteousness and strict moral code; it was to cause a lot of unnecessary suffering to innocent people.

Colchester town did not escape the ravages of war when in June 1648 an army of 6,000 Royalists marched towards the town. The citizens of Colchester were not pleased to find an army at their town gates.

At the head of this army was Sir Charles Lucas, a local man, and he soon persuaded the town to open the gates. Faced with overwhelming odds the townspeople let them in. The castle was by now in a poor state of repair and of no military importance to the Royalists, who used it to stable their horses and to shelter their wounded. Following in close pursuit was Thomas, Lord Fairfax, the Parliamentarian general who had defeated the Royalists in battle in Kent, and had pursued them through Essex to Colchester.

The citizens welcomed Fairfax and his army at first; later they had a different attitude towards him. The Royalists were now trapped in the town with the citizens. Fairfax set about surrounding the town with forts and camps, with cannon pointing towards the town walls.

After six days Fairfax had completed his task and the town was now under siege. Sir Charles Lucas led several sorties into the surrounding countryside for corn and cattle, and made some night attacks on the forts and camps, damaging some cannons. Lord Fairfax increased his patrols, strengthened the forts, and continually bombarded the town causing much damage to the town wall and houses. No person was allowed in or out of the town and food was becoming scarce.

The weather at this time was terrible, continual rain and very cold, which soon made life in the town unpleasant and very unsanitary. The people became ill and were reduced to scavenging for food, eating dogs and cats and anything else they could find, while the Royalists were reduced to killing and eating their horses. A contingent of women from the town went to the gates and pleaded with Fairfax to call off the siege and to let them leave the town, but their plight was ignored and the siege continued.

In August Sir Charles Lucas and Sir George Lisle realised that no help was at hand and that their situation was desperate. All around soldiers and civilian were dying, some from wounds sustained in battle, others who had succumbed to sickness or starvation. The siege had lasted for three months with continual bombardment from artillery, running battles at the walls and gates, and many buildings damaged. The time had come to surrender and a delegation was sent out of town to meet Lord Fairfax to discuss the terms. Both sides ceased hostilities while awaiting the outcome.

On Monday 28th August 1648 the terms were agreed and signed; the Royalists surrendered and the town gates opened. From the 6,000 men who went into the town only 3,531 remained, many of them sick and dying. Fairfax marched in and immediately arrested the senior Royalists leaders; George, Lord Goring, Sir Charles Lucas, Sir George Lisle, Sir Bernard Gascoigne and Arthur, Lord Capel. They were brought before Fairfax and his generals, told they were to be executed and were then led away and held in the castle to await their fate. Later that evening soldiers arrived at the door of the prison where the Royalists leaders were being held; they marched them out of the castle and made them stand near the north wall, several lines of musketeers stood before the condemned men. Sir Charles Lucas was told he was to die first, moments later shots rang out and he fell dead. Then Sir George Lisle was led to the spot where his friend lay, he knelt down, kissed the body and said farewell in prayer, minutes later he too was dead, the two men who fought together in battle now died together in defeat.

The other Royalist leaders were reprieved from the death sentence, but Lord Goring and Lord Capel were tried by Parliament, and later executed at the Tower of London. Sir Bernard Gascoigne was reprieved and allowed to leave as he was an Italian, and Fairfax did not want to start a diplomatic incident by having him executed. The bodies of Lucas and Lisle were taken to St Giles church and buried quietly and without ceremony. Later a commemorative slab was placed in the church with the words, UNDER THIS MARBLE LY THE BODIES OF THE TWO MOST VALIANT CAPTAINS SR CHARLES LVCAS AND SR GEORGE LISLE KNIGHTS, WHO FOR THEIR EMINENT LOYALTY TO THEIR SOVEREIN WERE ON THE 28TH DAY OF AVGVST 1648 BY THE COMMAND OF SR THOMAS FAIRFAX, THEN GENERAL OF THE PARLIAMENT ARMY, IN COLD BLOOD BARBAROVSLY MVRDERD.

An obelisk to the North of the castle was erected in 1883 and marks the spot of the execution of Lisle and Lucas. Tradition says that no grass will grow on the spot, and as it is now paved over the tradition lives on! Meanwhile the Parliamentarian army moved into the town and set about rounding up the Royalist soldiers and robbing them of anything of value. Many were sick, so were shot on the spot and left lying in the street; the others were marched away and imprisoned or sent to serve sentences in the West Indies.

The town had suffered badly in the siege. Apart from the people losing their homes and being sick from starvation, trade had been affected by the war and many faced financial ruin. Many of the town's ancient buildings were damaged or destroyed by cannon fire. St Botolph's 12th century priory was a victim, along with several church towers and parts of the old town walls. Over 180 houses were in ruins and the many dead were given hasty burials. Fairfax imposed a heavy fine on the town, mostly to pay for the army; some money was given to Dutch immigrants who lived in the town whose trade had suffered in the siege. The citizens were left with the job of cleaning up and rebuilding the town, and it was many years before the town recovered from the siege and the fine.

The castle was now in a dilapidated state. The roof had gone, but some chambers were still used to hold prisoners. The castle had been sold by the Crown in 1649, and was now in private hands. The owner in 1656 was Sir James Norfolk. At this time the Quaker preacher, James Purnell, was imprisoned in the castle for disorderly conduct at a church service in Colchester, and was jailed for refusing to pay a fine. He was held in conditions that were so bad that he died of the hardships that were imposed on him; he was just 20 years old.

Many years later the prison reformer John Howard was reporting and recording the conditions in the castle. He was appalled at the conditions he found here and at other jails around the country, but it was to be another 200 years before the castle was finally closed as a prison forever.

In the years following the death of James Purnell, the Norfolk family maintained the castle, finally selling it to John Wheely, a local ironmonger, in 1683 for the purpose of demolishing the castle and selling stone. Wheely set about the task of demolition with gusto, starting at the top, dismantling the stone with gangs of men using hammers, but this proved too slow so he resorted to using gunpowder! Large chunks of masonry fell to the floors below cracking open the base of the castle to reveal the vaults of the Roman temple, filled with sand. Wheely switched from dismantling the stone to removing the sand hoping that he might find Roman treasure; he could also sell the sand at the same time. The Roman arched vaults supported the weight of the original temple , and then the Norman castle; the sand was an integral part of the design for both structures. By starting to remove the sand Wheely caused huge cracks to appear in the vaults, rendering the whole structure unsafe.

At this point he gave up the enterprise as too costly and sold the castle in 1704 to Sir Isaac Rebow, MP for Colchester. By now the castle had lost the top two storeys. It had no roof, and would be called today a 'picturesque ruin'. It later came into the hands of Charles Gray MP for Colchester, who turned out to be the castle's saviour. Gray and his wife acquired it as a gift from his mother-in-law, Mrs Mary Webster, who bought the castle in 1727 from Charles Rebow, grandson of Sir Isaac. Mrs Webster lived at Castle House (now Holly Trees Museum) until her death in 1754, when Gray became the sole owner of the castle. Charles Gray set about restoring and repairing the damaged stone work of the south wing, building the first floor arcade, roofing over the crypt enlarging the windows on the south wall, and creating a library and private museum. He built the domed tower over the great staircase, where later a tree was planted to commemorate the battle of Waterloo, 18th June 1815.

Charles Gray was Colchester's MP for 30 years, a lawyer by profession and a Fellow of the Royal Society. He also established the *Castle Society,* a group of like minded individuals who were interested in the preservation of the past and its antiquities. Gray worked on the restoration of the castle until his death in 1782. He is buried in All Saints Church (now the Natural History Museum) opposite the castle he helped save from destruction. There is a portrait of Charles Gray in the Holly Trees Museum. The castle now became the property of the Round family of Birch Hall, who maintained the work that Gray had started. The castle became a public museum in 1860 when Charles Gray Round, MP for North Essex, brought various collections of antiquities from private collectors and some from the Essex Archæological Society, and put them together under one roof in the crypt of the castle. Eventually in 1920 the collection was given to the Borough of Colchester by Viscount Cowdray, High Steward of Colchester, and the last private owner of the castle.

Problems started to appear in the Roman vaults in 1933 when cracks were found in the ceiling, due to rain water seeping in from the open area of the castle keep. The vaults' ceilings were repaired, and the decision was made to roof over the entire keep, to save the vaults from further damage. Work on the interior was completed when new galleries were constructed to house the expanding collection of Roman antiquities. The refurbished castle, complete with roof and new galleries, was officially opened in 1935.

At this time excavations were taking place outside the castle to the south side of the keep, they revealed the foundations of a 12th century building. It was probably a protective gate or barbican to the original entrance into the keep. The foundations of a chapel were also found. An oak bridge was constructed to the main entrance over the excavations, that is in use today, and takes the visitor into the museum. The castle was used to protect local people during the second world war, when the vaults were opened as an air raid shelter, 1939-45.

The castle today is one of the best examples of an early stone Norman castle, and is the largest castle keep in Europe. It houses a fine collection of Celtic and Roman artefacts, found in and around the town. Especially interesting are two fine Roman tombstones. One depicts a centurion in the uniform of an officer from the 20th Legion, he was called *Marcus Favonius Facilis,* a man of rank. Even carved in stone he has the air of extreme confidence befitting a Roman officer. He is seen holding a wooden staff *(vitis),* a symbol of his rank, and his left hand rests on his sword. The other tombstone depicts a mounted cavalry officer whose name was *Longinus Sdapeze.* It shows him seated on his horse trampling over a submissive Celtic fighting man. This stone was badly damaged when found in 1928; and although it was restored by the museum, the face was missing from the mounted figure. In 1996 while the Essex Archæological Society was excavating the site where the tombstone was originally found, the missing face was found, to everyone's joy and surprise. So now after 900 years the restoration of the face to the tombstone will be made by the museum, and will be on show for all to see.

The museum is in the care of Colchester Borough Council who have many rich and fine objects to care for. Celtic and Roman coins, ancient coffins, pottery and models. A walk round the museum will take you through all ages of history, and in the prison you can even listen to the voices of the past. A castle guide takes parties into the Roman vaults and then on to the roof to look over the old bailey and the town. On a sunny day the castle positively glows. With its red roof, red Roman tiles and honey stone walls, it looks very Mediterranean, and is some times mistaken for a Roman brick building. But it is very Norman, built by Normans on a Roman site re-using Roman brick and tiles. The castle we see today is only half the height it once was, and the bailey and earthworks are now incorporated into Castle Park, but nevertheless the keep is one of the most impressive monuments of Norman rule you will see anywhere.

For further information telephone 01206 282931/2.

WALDEN CASTLE
OS 154   TL 5439

Walden castle sits crumbling and forlorn in the grounds of the local museum. Abandoned by its owners many years ago, the stone taken by local people, leaving the shell of a once great home and castle. It is fenced off to protect the public from falling masonry with a 'Beware' notice on the wall.

The visitor can walk around the outside, and wonder what life may have been like inside the castle during the 12th century when it was built. The name Walden is from the Saxon word *wald* or *weala dean* meaning woodland and valley. Saffron is from the plant, *Crocus Sativus* which was grown in the area between 1400 and 1700.

The manor was held by Ausgar, master of horse to Edward the Confessor. Later it was given to Geoffrey de Mandeville who came to England with William the Conqueror in 1066 and was given many estates in Essex and Hertfordshire. Walden castle was commissioned by Geoffrey de Mandeville II, son of William de Mandeville and grandson to the first Geoffrey.

The first reference to the castle was made in 1141, when Geoffrey II was given permission by the Empress Maud to move a market from the nearby village of Newport to his new castle at Walden.

The England of 1141 was place of strife for the nation; and a time of opportunity for men like Geoffrey de Mandeville II. A civil war was taking place between supporters of King Stephen and the daughter of Henry I, Matilda, also known as the Empress Maud. The problem was, that before Henry died, he made the barons promise to accept Matilda as queen, as his only son, William, had drowned in the *White Ship* disaster in 1120.

When Henry died, in 1135, Matilda was out of the country. Her cousin, Stephen, was accepted by the barons as king, as many were not prepared to have a queen as monarch. So supporters from each side were ready to fight for their own candidate and Geoffrey II took full advantage of the situation, playing both sides against each other. However, after he promised to support Matilda in 1143, Stephen forced Geoffrey to surrender his castles at Walden and Pleshey to the crown, setting Geoffrey on the road to ruin, and later death in battle.

In the reign of Henry II, 1154-89, the castle was restored to Geoffrey de Mandeville III, but within two years the castle was partly demolished on the order of the king. The town, now called *Chipping* or *Chepying Walden,* started to grow around the market and the castle, and by the 14th century was established as a wool and weaving area, with the added skill of dyeing, using the saffron plant which was cultivated in local gardens. The plant flourished because of the ideal soil mixture of dry clay and chalk, it also provided cures for the townpeoples' ailments, and flavouring for their food

By the 16th century the town called itself Saffron Walden. The saffron flower was incorporated into the town's coat of arms granted in 1549 by King Edward VI. Eventually the industry declined; finally abandoned in the 18th century. Brewing then replaced weaving and dyeing. Malting had been established since the reign of Richard II, and continued until the 19th century; the last malting firm working until quite recently in the town.

The castle was built of flint and stone rubble, mixed with mortar for strength, and perhaps faced with ashlar stone similar to Castle Hedingham. It was a substantial dwelling three storeys high, with the basement at ground level. An earth mound was around the base of the keep; the basement must have been cold and dark; probably used for storage. Above was a hall with fireplaces and another room above the hall, probably sleeping quarters. There was a stairway to the upper.and lower rooms. A well shaft approximately 75 feet in depth provided the castle with its water supply; traces of the shaft can be seen in the north west corner of the keep. The remains of a large stone pillar (now only a metre high) can be seen in the centre of the keep, but when the castle was constructed it extended to at least the first floor as a support.

Outside a forebuilding was built against the outerwall with a staircase and ramp that led to the main entrance at first floor level. Surrounding the keep would be earth banks and ditches of the inner bailey, the line can be traced and follows Museum Street, Castle Street, and Church Street.

After Geoffrey de Mandeville's death the castle passed to the de Saye family who were second cousins, but they were unable to maintain the castle so it passed to Geoffrey FitzPiers II, also a cousin.

The castle was not lived in on a regular basis for many years, until 1346, when the de Bohun family were given permission to fortify the castle with battlements. A hall and other smaller buildings were constructed in the inner and outer baileys. The castle was taken by the crown in 1362 after the de Bohun family quarrelled with the king, Edward III. The castle remained the property of the crown until the reign of Henry VIII.

The estate was given by the king to Sir Thomas Audley and, after his death, to his daughter Margaret, who married the Duke of Norfolk, a member of the Howard family. It was Thomas Howard, son of the fourth Duke of Norfolk who over the years received many titles and honours, and concentrated his energy into building Audley End house, on the site of Walden Priory built by Geoffrey de Mandeville in 1140. It became a Benedictine abbey in 1190. Nothing remains of the abbey above ground today. When Audley End House was completed it was one of the architectural wonders of the age, built in the Anglo-Flemish style. The castle was ignored while the great house was admired.

Over the years Walden Castle gradually lost its importance, and fell into disrepair; the stone taken away to make roads and used locally to build houses. By 1790 the castle was a complete ruin.

Some walls were demolished to build a barn and a small farm , and an entrance made wider to enable horse wagons to enter. Later a round turret was built on the north west corner by the 1st Lord Braybrooke for possible use as a signal station in the event of Napoleon's threatened invasion. A flag pole was later attached to the tower and remained there for many years until it was blown down in a storm. The interior of the castle was cleared of the farm and old barn in 1881. A sword and some other small items were found in the ruins of the old castle; they are now in the museum for safe keeping.

The castle gradually faded in to a shapeless hulk, sheep grazed around its walls, and birds nested in the masonry.

The museum next to the castle has been established and open to the public since 1835 and has collected many fine objects of interest. It was later suggested that the castle could be an extension to the museum, and several heavy items. including stone coffins and an old wooden pillory were set up inside the castle. However, there was no cover as the castle was open to all weathers; a suggestion was considered to roof over the castle, but this came to nothing.

In 1932, to celebrate the centenary of a local society a musical concert was held inside the ruins of the castle attracting a large audience, probably enjoying the music but with one eye watching the weather!

In 1979 the Neville family passed Walden Castle on to Uttlesford District Council who are responsible for its care and have the task of presenting it to the people as an historic artefact. They have a problem as the shell of the castle is in a poor state of repair after years of neglect. Some repairs to the wall were made in 1980, but at the moment it is best described as a picturesque ruin.

The castle is a Scheduled Ancient Monument, and a worthy building to have in any town. An excellent guide to the castle is published by the Saffron Waiden Museum; and is on sale in the museum, next to the castle ruins

Walden Castle and Saffron Walden Museum

MISCELLANEOUS MOTTES

Abandoned mottes are dotted around the countryside; they are grass-covered mounds of earth, topped with trees that seem to grip the earth beneath them in case they are blown away. They vary in size from a 20 feet high mound at Great Easton to 65 feet in height at Thetford in Norfolk.

The motte and bailey type castle spread throughout Britain in the 11th century, guarding the land that had been taken from the defeated Saxons and given to a Norman baron.

Motte and bailey castles were usually built near rivers or on the edge of villages, using the natural contours of the land, small hills and ancient earthworks, abandoned long before the Normans arrived.

This is where the invaders lived after 1066, men and horses living together in a little community, always on the alert in case of rebellion from the Saxons, but they were uncomfortable and vulnerable to attack and fire. They were soon abandoned for more substantial dwellings of stone, and by the 12th century the great age of castle building was well established in Britain, instigated by the Normans.

Very little written history exists about the minor mottes. The historian can measure the height and width, dig for artefacts, then move on to more exciting finds in the ground; leaving the mounds to nature and for future generations to wonder what these bumps in the countryside were, and ponder over their history.

In Essex there are several small mounds, some that are on private land and cannot be seen without the owners' consent; others can be seen from footpaths or from the road.

At GREAT EASTON (OS 167 TL6125) there is a small motte in the grounds of Easton Hall circular in shape, 20 feet high, flat-topped and approximately 130 feet in diameter. It has a dry ditch that  surrounds the mound, this is quite shallow only 4 to 5 feet deep. Excavations were carried out in Victorian times on the mound, and some slight damage was caused at the time. The bailey has been completely destroyed over the years by ploughing and farming. The mound is typically Norman and in 1086 when the Domesday Book was compiled, the Norman Matthew of Mortagne, was the owner of Great Easton. It was taken from a freeman named Aki, who owned the land before 1066. The value then was ten pounds, beyond that no other information can be found. The mound is on private lands but can be seen through a hedge, near the road that runs through the village.

###

Another small mound is at RICKLING (OS 167 TL 5030), 20 feet high with a dry moat. It is on private land in the grounds of Rickling Hall, a 15th century manor house. This estate was called Richelinga, and belonged to King Harold in 1066.

After the conquest and the death of Harold the estate went to King William. The size of the mound and moat would suggest that a large wooden tower and palisade were constructed, with a large outer bailey.

The estate and motte were later owned by Geoffrey de Mandeville who held castles at Pleshey and nearby Walden. When Henry III came to the throne, many of the old castles were demolished to reduce the power of feudal knights, it is probable that Rickling castle went at this time.

The mound today cannot be seen by the public due to its private location in Rickling Hall garden; there is no public footpath nearby.

###

At STEBBING (OS 167 TL 6624) a large 44 feet high circular motte is surrounded by a water filled moat. It is on private land, but can be seen from a public foot path that runs along the east side of the motte. Before 1066 the land was owned by Siward, a freeman; then it was taken by William and given to the Norman, Henry of Ferrers, who along with Ranulf Peverel were recorded as the new land owners in 1086. No date can be put on the mound, but as with the previous mounds it would have served the same purpose for the Normans.

88

Stebbing is particularly attractive in the spring when the mound is covered in daffodils, and ducks swim on the moat.

A substantial mount is at MOUNT BURES (OS 933 TL 9033), north of Colchester, sited behind the church of St John, built in what's left of the outer bailey. The tree covered mound is  approximately 40 feet high, and 200 feet round at the base, standing in a dry ditch or moat in the same early Norman castle style. It was probably constructed soon after the Norman occupation.

When the Domesday survey was conducted in 1086, the land was owned by Roger of Poitou, later passing to King Henry I, who then let the land to the Sackville family, who had to lease the land from King Stephen (1135-54).

The fate of the castle is unknown, possibly abandoned for something more secure and comfortable. It is a fine example of a motte and ditch, the inner and outer baileys normally associated with this type of dwelling are no longer discernible.

A smaller motte can be found at ELMDON (OS 154 TL 4640), but this is on private land and cannot be seen. Aelmer, a freeman, held the land before 1066, it was then given to Roger de Sommery, from Count Eustace of Boulogne.

Many mottes over the years have been lost to farming, erosion, and building. The county is lucky to have so many remnants of the Norman occupation scattered about the countryside. So much has been lost over the years to the ever expanding population, and the need for land to build on. The larger stone Norman buildings are in safe hands - preserving them for future generations, but the vulnerable mounds - what future have they?

Those on private property should be safe, but the need for land could make them expendable, after all they are only mounds of earth with trees growing on them, not a lot to see, and the word 'castle' does not immediately spring to mind; but they are the remnants of an occupation by a foreign invader nearly a thousand years ago that changed England forever.

The earthworks at Stanstead are a splendid example of what can be done. By turning an abandoned earthwork into a reconstructed Norman village, it brings to life the earth and grass, with buildings and stories of what life may have been like all those years ago.

SOURCES

A Dictionary of British History *J P Kenyon*   Secker & Warburg

The Dictionary of National Biography   Oxford University Press

Domesday book. 32 Essex   Phillimore

England under the Normans 1066-1154 *G Wilson* R H Fowler

Essex under arms *Ken Smith*   Ian Henry

Cassell's History of England, Vol 1   Cassell

Kings and Queens of Britain *D. Williamson*   Webb & Bower

The King's England. Essex. *Arthur Mee*   Hodder & Stoughton

The People's History of Essex *D W Coller*   Meggy & Chalk, Chelmsford

Resist the Invader *P R Gifford*   Essex Libraries

1066 The year of the Conquest *David Howarth*   R Clark

The entrance to Hedingham Castle

INDEX
Items in **bold** show major chapters